Vitas Gerulaitis: Portrait

By Scoop Malinowski

Copyright 2024 by Mark Scoop Malinowski

Cover photo by Fred Mullane

All Rights Reserved

ISBN: 9798878766654

Beginnings are always difficult. And the origin of inspiration for this book is unusual. I had just one fleeting encounter with tennis titan Vitas Gerulaitis... I walked by him as he sat on a couch by himself one afternoon at the US Open player's lounge in 1993. Looking for subjects to do a Biofile interview for my syndicated newspaper column, I made a quick decision to decline to approach Vitas for an interview which I'm now certain he would have kindly done with this young, nobody reporter. I still remember the reason why - He was associated with drugs.

It was a regrettably stupid judgment in hindsight. I wish I did the Biofile with Vitas that day because he was one of the most unique figures of tennis history.

Decades later a tennis friend named Rob Glickman

repeatedly urged me to do a book on his old friend Vitas, in the format of my other tennis books on Roger Federer, Marcelo Rios, John McEnroe, Novak Djokovic, Bjorn Borg.

Initially, this idea was rejected. Vitas is forgotten, nobody cares. But then I started to hear stories about his extraordinary qualities of kindness, generosity, friendly nature, popularity and ability to interact with the super famous and ordinary Joe.

Maybe a long feature story about Vitas would be interesting. That idea eventually evolved into this book...

The generous, charismatic, beloved "Lithuanian Lion" from Queens, New York once inspired a dear friend to say: "Vitas wouldn't give you the shirt off his back if you needed it, he'd go home and get you a clean one."

Vytautas Kevin Gerulaitis was born on July 26, 1954 in Brooklyn, NY. Taught by his father who was a tennis instructor, "Vitas" played one year at Columbia University in New York before embarking in 1971 on a successful professional tennis career, highlighted by winning the 1977 Australian Open title vs John Lloyd 63 75 57 36 62, playing in the US Open final of 1980 vs. John McEnroe and the 1980 Roland Garros final vs. Bjorn Borg. Gerulaitis won 26 overall ATP singles titles and eight more in doubles including 1975 Wimbledon doubles title with Sandy Mayer. His highest career ranking was ATP no. 3 in February 1978.

After his playing career, which ended in 1986, Gerulaitis became a successful TV analyst for USA Network from 1988-1994. He also coached Jimmy Connors and Pete Sampras during the 1994 Italian Open, due to Pete's regular coach Tim Gullikson being on a family vacation. Sampras won the final in Rome vs Boris Becker in straight sets.

Just days after the 1994 US Open, Gerulaitis tragically died in Southampton, New York, while sleeping in a guesthouse of a friend, due to carbon monoxide poisoning.

This book is a collection of memories, stories and anecdotes about one of the most unique, popular and adored champions in tennis history...

Eugene L. Scott: Since it can be argued that Arthur Ashe was one of the game's greatest men, in the purest sense of the word, and Lew Hoad was one of the greatest players, can there be a challenge to Vitas Gerulaitis having the most personality?

With Vitas' passing, some of the misplaced conclusions about his accomplishments can be corrected for the record. The notion that his fast lane life prevented him from reaching No. 1 is preposterous. That he won Australian Open, won the Wimbledon doubles and reached a career high ranking of no. 3 is a tribute to his hard work, quickness and all-around athletic ability, not to his shotmaking or technique.

Vitas himself would agree that his second service belonged on the women's tour, although he was unusually resourceful in covering up this particular weakness. While his speed at net and in the backcourt had the effect on opposition of being caught in the middle of a laser light show, he had no overpowering weapon to control a match. He won by outworking and outcompeting the other guy.

People forget that on the occasions Vitas stayed out too late, he would still pay an unholy price in the next day on the practice court. The Borg-Gerulaitis eight-hour, eight-set workouts were legendary. Other players would actually duck them as practice partners, so grueling were there sessions.

Personal observations on Vitas... I like the one Mary Carillo told at Vitas' funeral about his World Team Tennis days in Pittsburgh. Once after a match, Vitas took the microphone and announced to a crowd of 6,000 that it was his birthday and everyone was invited to a pajama party at his hotel. Vitas hired the room, the booze and a band, got into his pajamas and waited. No one came. Feeling depressed, he fetched a drink, paced around the room forlorn, looked out the window. There in the parking lot below were 1,000 people in their pajamas, holding candles. The mother of all birthday parties ensued.

Vitas was the personification of the pied piper. Everyone wanted to be in his company and the everyone was ageless and genderless. He had the knack of making those around him feel important. Most of us don't have that level of tolerance. Momma Gerulaitis and sister Ruta knew some in the coterie were creeps. But Vitas never minded – he didn't want to hurt anyone's feelings.

The glare off Gerulaitis did not come from the Simoniz on his Rolls Royce but it did obscure his earnestness to do good. Did you know, for instance, Vitas was the first of the stars to start his own foundation to teach inner city kids how to play tennis? In 1977 he founded the Vitas Gerulaitis Foundation and over the next ten years his organization gave away 40,000 free racquets primarily for his New York City Parks programs.

He commandeered friends including Borg, McEnroe and Vilas to donate their time for summer lessons. And whenever friends asked him to reciprocate for their own pro/celebrity cause, he was the first to R.S.V.P.

Shall we say the Gerulaitis funeral was not orchestrated with marching band precision? Such regimen would have been inappropriate to the ruling whimsy of Vitas' life. What we did see was a spontaneous outpouring of affection. No plans. Everyone pitched in their personal tributes without coaxing. Chris Evert flew from Colorado. Janet Jones from California. Nike's Ian Hamilton from Seattle. Billie Jean King from Chicago. And Vitas broadcasting sidekick Pat O'Brien managed a red-eye from the west coast.

The Long Island Expressway was closed by state troopers for the half dozen exits along the procession from the church to the burial site. Presidents get that kind of salute.

Vitas was buried with his favorite five-iron, a blank scorecard and a few tees. Perhaps just the tools for heavenly doglegs. Or a sad reminder that this man was under-clubbed on his way to the green.

Contributors

Eugene L. Scott

Chris Lewis

Harold Mollin

Don Petrine

Steven Yellin

Brian Teacher

Kim Clayton

Van Winitsky

Trey Waltke

Rick Fagel

John James

Koko

Dan McClure

Chris Sylvan

Jeff Chambers

Jay Volek

Robert Palmer

John Rast

Bill Koegler

Brad Gilbert

Bunner Smith

Brian Gottfried

Hans Gildemeister

Jan Triska

Gene Mayer

Ed Wolfarth

Fred Stolle

John Cavanaugh

Lisa Kerkorian

Kyle Johnson

Rob Glickman

Bjorn Borg

Jimmy Connors

Joy DeVijon

Ken Williams

Glenn Muller

Carl Vaughn

Jonathan Chimene

Timothy Vann

Lee Morris

Jeffrey Scott

Gregory Nimensky

Luigi Stasi

John Lloyd

Ruta Gerulaitis

Patrick McEnroe

Steve Flink

Andy Warhol

Shelby Rogers

Pete Sampras

Tim Mayotte

John McEnroe

Steve Tignor

Bob Lutz

Johan Kriek

Leif Shiras

Barry Beck

Andres Gomez

Fritz Buehning

Fred Mullane

Ilie Nastase

Nancy Gill McShea

Pat Cash

LeRoy Neiman

Peter Figura

VITAS GERULAITIS: Portrait Of A Champion

Chris Lewis: Before commenting on his game, I would like to say a few things about Vitas, the person. On the tour, he was universally liked. Flamboyant, charismatic, witty and incredibly generous, Vitas was always great company, with a tremendous sense of life. With Vitas, there NEVER was a dull moment. Whether it was watching his favorite sports teams, heading out to Studio 54 in his Rolls Royce or practicing for the US Open at his Long Island home, Vitas enjoyed himself. He lived life as if every second counted. And he was popular because wherever he went, he was always in good humor. People loved being around him, and he them.

For example, even though he wasn't exactly an embodiment of the values represented by that golden era of Australian tennis, when Australia ruled the tennis world, he was well liked by the Australian greats. For instance, he got on tremendously well with Fred Stolle and I know that Tony Roche also thought highly of Vitas and you only had to look at who attended his funeral to see how highly regarded he was by his contemporaries. As far as his playing goes, he definitely was NOT a subscriber to 'The Seles Principle.' He was no 800 lb. gorilla, his game had no 'heft.' It was a game built purely around speed and reflexes - lightning quick foot speed and even faster cat-like reflexes. He was also an extremely quick thinker and decision maker, making full use of a limited arsenal to exploit any of his opponents' weaknesses. He was also a guy who wasn't scared to take the initiative by coming in behind a relatively weak second serve, backing himself - and his speed - to worry the guy into making a return error. You need a special sort of courage to do that.

His was a game that said: "pass me or lob me fifty times in the next two hours and the match is yours." Bjorn could do it, Jimmy could do it, Ivan could do it, John could do it, but there weren't too many others who could do it often enough to beat him consistently. To quote Peter Bodo, 'Vitas was a player who fits into the, One thing I'm confident about, though, is that it's pretty easy to overlook the value of speed and quickness. Give me a player with world class speed (and I'm talking track-and-field world class), consistent groundstrokes, and a strong mind and - bingo! - he's Top 5 for sure category. In Vitas' case, it wasn't that he relied on consistent groundstrokes and his speed around the baseline to win matches, even though he did this well when he couldn't get in, he relied on consistent volleys and his speed around the net. I think another factor in Vitas' on-court success was his larger than life off-court status; he was a true celebrity in the tennis' rock 'n roll era. Didn't matter where he was, walking down the streets of Manhattan, dining in a fashionable restaurant in London or stepping on to the Concorde in Paris, Vitas turned heads. He was the guy who hung out with guys like Mick Jagger and dated Vogue cover supermodels like Janet Jones. Like Bjorn, Vitas brought fans through the gate. Crowds wanted him to win. Most of the time, the guys he played just didn't have nearly the same status, nor the same star quality. A born showman, Vitas nearly always established a very positive rapport with the spectators. He engaged them. They wanted to see HIM play the next day, not the other poor sap. He was exciting to watch. Is this a factor in a tennis match... the psychological factor involved when playing a BIG name? You bet -- unless you're one of those anti-hero types who likes to spoil the script by ruining the ending. Didn't happen that often, though. Just against the very best. Like the sixteen times in a row he was beaten by Jimmy and upon finally beating him for the first time, Vitas' immortal words to the press were, "Nobody beats Vitas Gerulaitis seventeen times in a row." Classic Vitas!

I mentioned in an earlier post that I practiced extensively with Vitas. Just a word about that. On the practice court, Vitas was all business. His work ethic - he was a Harry

Hopman protégé - was flawless. He was easily one of the Tour's most hard-working, conscientious players on the practice court. Tireless, even after a VERY late night, or nights. Like everything he did, he loved to play. He was one of the few guys who actually ENJOYED pushing himself to the max in practice, and then heading off for some interval training afterwards. Nicknamed "Broadway Vitas" by the press, he lived life in the fast lane, all the time. To me, his legacy is that of someone who squeezed out every ounce of life before his accidental and tragic death. He was both a great player and a great person.

Gerulaitis won head to head series 2-0

1981 Tokyo Indoor   Carpet   R16   Gerulaitis
      6-2 6-3

1981 Melbourne Indoor Carpet   SF Gerulaitis
      6-4 6-1

Harold Mollin: Vitas and I would practice every day for over a year when I would pick him up at his Howard Beach Home, and then we would either go to Port Washington Tennis Academy at 5:00 am - free time for us - or some public outdoor courts in Manhattan on the East River. He was relentless. And when he was fifteen, and I was eighteen, we won the Men's Eastern Hardcourt Championships held in Long Island's Woodbury Country Club. No one believed we could win it since my skills were limited to a serve, and some quickness - and there were many ex-Davis Cup players living around New York who were playing this tournament. And, most obviously, Vitas was only fifteen. After upsetting everyone from the first round onwards, we played a great final against a Cuban Davis Cup player, and established veterans champion as his partner. To make a long story short, that fifteen year old carried his partner to victory by his amazing volleying, returns, and incessant banter. He was THE BEST!

Don Petrine: Incredible guy, man. Incredible guy. The most charismatic player ever, besides his best friend Bjorn Borg. I played on the Columbia University team with him when he was there for the one year he was at the school. He was a freshman, I was a sophomore. His best friend was Rick Fagel, they traveled together for ten years or so. He's got stories that he told me that I didn't experience like Vitas spent a half a million dollars at Bjorn Borg's bachelor party. Vitas was a very smart guy. On the SAT test he scored 1550 out of 1600. He had incredible energy.

My first memory of Vitas is I didn't know him at the time I went to Easter Bowl, some of my friend knew him. At the time everyone was saying, You gotta see this kid Vitas play. He wasn't doing well yet. He wasn't playing a lot of junior tournaments. He got into Easter Bowl. Everybody knew he was going to be a great player. He had the perfect game for grass. Back then three of the Grand Slams were played on grass. On the junior tour I didn't know him but he was known as a big party animal. It was said he dealt drugs to finance his junior career. At that time the junior circuit was four cities - Louisville, St. Louis, Springfield, Ohio and Kalamazoo. In my opinion, he could do any kind of drugs and metabolize it. He had so much energy in his system that he could metabolize it. I went to Columbia my sophomore year and he was being recruited. He was Gene Scott's boy. Gene Scott took care of him.

Vitas was the only guy I ever saw who could play three times a day all out for three hours each time. All out. I saw him do it. I saw him play Orange Bowl, we were watching him play Borg in the quarterfinals. That was the first time we saw Borg. He lost to Borg in three sets. Walking off the court, Vitas said to his friends, 'Who was that guy? And what was THAT?' That was the beginning of the Borg-Vitas relationship. Borg played with a lot of top spin on both sides, which nobody has seen before, and he didn't miss a ball. You couldn't attack Borg and get him in trouble, he'd get to every ball. Vitas knew it. Vitas had variety but he wasn't expecting that. Borg had won the 16s the year before at Orange Bowl. But we didn't really see him play. He wasn't on the radar. His style was like he took Connors game and put top spin on the ball. I think Vilas was already gone. Vilas was a similar situation a few years before but Vilas was slicing every backhand. Vilas could make the ball dance through the air.

Vitas was a remarkable guy. If you look at the pallbearers at his funeral, no one really liked each other. Nut they all liked Vitas. Borg, Connors, McEnroe, but when it came to Vitas, they were all his friends.

I ran the Pro-Am Calcutta the the spring before he died, pros and amateurs and gambling on the matches. At Royal Palm Tennis Club in Pine Crest, FL. To raise money for the American Cancer Society. In order to get Vitas there I had to pick him up at Turnberry in a limousine, out of bed. He played the Calcutta. He had tons of charisma in abundance, that's for sure. Everybody was thrilled. He had that inter-personal skill with strangers. He didn't know anybody there but Rick Fagel and I. That was at the end, the spring before he died.

Vitas made tennis Hollywood. I remember he was doing TV commentary during the US Open. Connors was playing on court. And he was talking to Vitas in the booth during the match, 'Hey Vitas, can you believe what's going on down here!?' It was one of the coolest things I've ever seen.

Steven Yellin: I remember practicing with Vitas at the Easterns at Forest Hills one year. It must have been in the 16s. Good guy but I wasn't that impressed with his game - his ground strokes were not that penetrating. Well, that changed pretty quickly.

Brian Teacher: Vitas was like warm Beacon of Light he always shined bright.

Teacher won head to head series 3-0

1983 Munich WCT   Carpet   QF Teacher 6-7 6-2 6-3

1981 Las Vegas   Hard QF Teacher 6-4 7-5

1977 Sydney Outdoor   Grass SF Teacher 7-5 7-6 6-3

Kim Clayton: 1977 Australian Open final Vitas vs. John

Lloyd... watched that match, loved Vitas. I was thirteen at the time and wanted to marry him. I remember Vitas had bad cramps in that match

Van Winitsky: I have fond memories of training a couple of winter seasons under Fred Stolle with Vitas, Nick Saviano, and Rick Fagel, though most the time practice didn't get started till noon with Vitas [laughs]. We had a couple of encounters. One Italian Open he teased me about my girlfriend. She was hot. He did compliment me on my denim jean jacket look one year at Forest Hills. I've heard a few things on Vitas mostly positive especially media-wise but rare other opinions too. We were pretty cool with each other for sure. We played one time in Toronto, he won 61 63.

Gerulaitis won head to head series 1-0

1979 Toronto Outdoor Hard R32 Gerulaitis 61 63

Trey Waltke: Borg, Connors and McEnroe taught us all how to be better tennis players. But Vitas taught us how to be better humans.

Rick Fagel: My first encounter with Vitas was when we were playing the junior Davis Cup tryouts at Stanford. He was starting to make his name. He was a top ten player in the 16s then going against seventeen and eighteen year olds. Also there were Chico Hagey, John Whitlinger, Jeff Miller, George Handie, Raul Ramirez, Vic Amaya, Bob Kreiss. Then he went to college two years later at Columbia. I played doubles with him. Vitas didn't complete that one year at Columbia. He had an academic scholarship. He was very, very bright but he was focused on tennis and going big time. So his academics suffered. To explain it - he would drive in for classes from home on Long Island. And not be able to find a parking spot, so then he went to practice tennis somewhere outside New York City. Since he would never find parking spaces, his grades suffered. I think he had two Fs, three incompletes and a pass in Lithuanian, which he spoke fluently. He was an extremely bright person and obsessive, so focused on what he was doing whether it was tennis, music, golf, friends, people. He became obsessed with different things. He had the first charity of all the tennis players - Vitas Gerulaitis Foundation.

I beat him in singles in college in the ECAC finals, in a third set tiebreaker. He was unhappy about me beating him but he didn't hold it against me.

Later I trained a lot with Vitas in South Florida. He got a great deal on a condo at Turnberry in Aventura. McEnroe and Connors also lived at Turnberry. Harold Solomon and Eddie Dibbs also lived in the area. All the guys came to practice with Fred Stolle. Vitas had met Fred in I think 1977 in World Team Tennis with the Pittsburgh Triangles. Fred was a protege of Harry Hopman who developed Vitas in Port Washington. Hopman came to coach Vitas at US Open in his later years.

Vitas didn't sleep much back in his heyday... this is getting to the dark side a little bit. It's called a 'natural short sleeper.' They can go without sleep and then they binge sleep later. Natural short sleepers only need four hours of sleep. I think Vitas was like that. He said he only needed four hours. He'd go to sleep at 5 and get up at 9 and feel refreshed and do a full day of training. I saw him do that so many times. Go to bed at 3 or 5 and get his four hours sleep. Wake up and do his practice regime of two-on-one drills that Hopman pioneered. The two-on-one drills were central to everything. It was all about running. Vitas had amazing footwork. Two guys at net and Vitas would be running for three hours in the morning, three hours in the afternoon. He trained harder than anybody at that place. Vitas could train six or seven hours at an incredible pace. Connors did it four an hour and a half and stopped. All that hard work really paid off when Vitas beat Vilas in the finals of the Italian Open in Rome in five hours (67 76 67 64 62 in 1979). It was the first time Vitas beat Vilas.

After Vitas retired from tennis he was looking for healthier outlets. He got into golf. I'm not a golfer but in a year and a half Vitas was a scratch golfer. I remember one time he was in Houston at rehab and he played 18 holes of golf and took a lesson in the morning and then 18 holes and a lesson in the afternoon at a different golf club. That was Vitas and how obsessive he could be about something.

The happiest I ever saw Vitas after a win... he exulted in victory. If he won, it showed. I remember he beat Ivan Lendl at US Open grandstand (round of 16 in 1981 63 64 36 36 64). I watched it with Dick Savitt (former Wimbledon champion) and he said "these are the most punishing rallies in a random tennis match I've ever seen." So Vitas was ecstatic after that. He and Lendl didn't get along. I remember Vitas not getting along with only two players - Lendl and Fibak.

His most painful loss was probably to Borg in the semis of Wimbledon. I don't think that loss was that painful as Vitas practiced with Vitas the next day. Another tough one was when he was playing Lendl in the Masters final at Madison Square Garden (1981). I think Vitas had a match point or it was an important point and Lendl beaned him in the forehead with a forehand (it happened at 2-0 in the third set). I remember Fred said Vitas didn't play the same after that (lost to Lendl 76 62 67 26 46).

[Note: Lendl later said he sensed Vitas seemed dazed by that shot until 25 in the third set. Lendl also said he believes that comeback from the two set deficit vs. Vitas may have given him the confidence to come back from two sets down to McEnroe in their famous 1984 French Open final which was Lendl's first Grand Slam title win.]

Strangest match I remember Vitas playing was against Adriano Panatta in Rome (1978 round of 64). Vitas had beaten Panatta the year before in Rome in three sets (QF). Vitas was up 5-1 in the first set and lost that set (7-6). Then Vitas was up 5-2 in the second set and lost that set (7-5). That was when the crowds in Rome were crazy, they were throwing huge coins at the players. Solomon walked off the court. If the ball was in by a foot, they'd call it out. Vitas lost to Panatta, the Italian crowd would not let Panatta lose. In the final Borg got hit with a coin and then he picked it up and showed everybody, kept playing.

Vitas had the greatest respect for Connors. Over the years Jimmy has said a lot of nice, gracious things about Vitas. At the eulogy at the funeral, he said a lot of good things. One thing he said that stands out was "at the tournaments, the spectators came to see Borg or me but after the match they belonged to Vitas." The top players are typically lone wolves - Borg, Connors, McEnroe, Vilas - but they all said Vitas was their best friend in tennis. At the funeral, they weren't the closest of friends but at the end they were all hugging each other.

Vitas was generous to anybody. He had a practice scheduled in the afternoon with Vitas. Vitas was running late, we were at the Publix getting lunch. Jimmy was a stickler for being punctual. Vitas was late. And an old lady would stop him and talk about her grand kids, showing pictures, and Vitas would look at them and talk with her.

You couldn't pick up a tab either. Of course, he had more money. He'd take us shopping in Italy, he'd buy for everybody. I saw him take off a $4,000 leather jacket and give it to a girl.

Vitas could play tennis on a different plain. Like that match with Lendl at US Open. In practice he could do some mind-boggling things. Training with Fred with guys who were super fit, like Nick Saviano and Tim Wilkison. He could train so hard at such high intensity. Two-on-one drills non-stop for ten minutes. And then say, 'Somebody else go now, take a turn.' I actually blacked out after a couple of minutes of doing the two-on-one drill. I wasn't as good as they were, I was trying hard to impress. Vitas would go ten straight minutes and not even tire. How did he do that?

John James: It is a match I would like to forget. I had a very good tournament beating some higher ranked players and reaching the semis. Vitas beat me 6-0,6-0. Very embarrassing. Feature match on a Saturday afternoon. I remember I really played okay. He was just too good for me. I somewhat consoled myself by realizing that we had very similar styles of play. He was just much better at it. The other main thing I remember from the match was how quick he was. None of my shots were big enough to get anything by him. A side note. After I stopped touring I played a lot of tournaments in the New York area. Many of those were held at the National Tennis Center where Vitas Gerualitis Sr. was a coach. He regularly came to watch my matches and chat afterwards. Very nice person. I was flattered that he took an interest in my tennis when he had a son who was such a great player.

Gerulaitis won head to head series 1-0

1979 Little Rock   Hard SF Gerulaitis 6-0 6-0

Koko: Vitas would come by Harry Hopman's Academy when it was in Bardmoor. He would train with some kids but mainly with guys like Andres Gomez and other pros who were in town training or staying in the area. During these practices, the juniors would stand and watch them practice. Vitas would always have a joke, good story to tell, or just ask us how we were playing. We thought he was a great guy and all of us looked up to him. He was a colorful character. Vitas would play some hilarious gags on players, coaches, whoever was around but he was always in a good mood and was really cool. Sometimes he'd hit with you but basically he never made you feel like you didn't belong. As I grew older and moved to London, his reputation lived almost as high a life as Vitas did himself.

Dan McClure: Vitas played on my high school team for one year at St. Andrews in Boca Raton. He came down for one year from New York. We never figured out why he came to play high school tennis in Florida for one year. We played doubles together and we beat Harold Solomon and a weaker player. I remember Vitas moved different, like a cat, he had this slinky way of moving around the court which made him a better player. He was a great guy, he was fun to hang out with, no arrogance at all. He never acted like he was "all that" even though he was "all that."

Chris Sylvan: I beat Gene Mayer and in the final Peter Fleming at the Eastern Junior Championships Under 14s in Forest Hills, NY. Gene was "the God" of the under 14s and later became ATP world no. 4. Peter won multiple Grand Slams in doubles. I attribute my success in that tournament to practicing with an obscure young teenager who was a year older. The guy played fantastic tennis but had no ranking at that time and didn't play in the tournament. He just practiced at the facility under the tutelage of pro Warren Woodcock. I remember saying to him, 'You have to play in these tournaments, you're way too good not to.' He didn't seem interested - at all. Well, about a year later, he was ranked nationally in the junior top five. His name? Vitas Gerulaitis.

Jeff Chambers: I played him at Hopman's Academy in Largo, Florida when he was top 5 in the world. I remember he was extremely quick and he trained very hard. And then after training on the court, he would go ride his bike for about 40 miles.

Jay Volek: Love Vitas. He was a lovely human being. I ballboyed for him in Durban, South Africa when I was fourteen. I ballboyed him a couple matches that week but it was awesome watching him take Connors apart after he had been partying late at Raffles night club the night before. He arrived at the locker rooms, his hair a mess, lipstick still smeared on his cheeks and smelling like a distillery. A 90 minute full body massage, quick shower and he walked out on the court fresh as a daisy. It was mind-boggling as I didn't think he would last a game the state he walked in. He regaled us ballboys with stories of him and McEnroe growing up and what a schmuck Connors was. I distinctly remember Vitas telling us how lazy McEnroe was to train because he was just so naturally talented and could get away with it. He was so nice and down to earth with us ball kids with zero airs and graces. A real mensch.

Question: What year was this?

Jay Volek: That would have been 1982 I believe at Westridge Park Tennis Stadium in Durban. My late father was a Davis Cup umpire and was friendly with Frew McMillan and the crowd from that era including Rod Laver and his amazing Aussie group.

Question: Any details of Connors being a schmuck?

Jay Volek: Let's just say as the ballboy at the net I was privy to some rather unsavory comments he made about his opponents just out of earshot of the umpire but not his opponent. He certainly was intimidating and I think the correct adjective was a bit salty. However, that was probably the gladiator in him because he was very decent in the change room. His fighting, never-say-die spirit was inspirational though especially to a tennis mad, impressionable teenager. But Vitas was my guy.

Question: Thanks for these details but what I meant actually was what Vitas said about Connors being a schmuck?

Jay Volek: I can't remember and I think it was just the saltiness factor and probably the same reason McEnroe called Jimbo an asshole. He wasn't a Vitas with his fellow players which is probably why he was a lot more successful than him.

Robert Palmer: In the 70s, a friend named John Rast worked his way into the 16s in the prestigious Kalamazoo junior tennis tournament. He did not have the support of his family and took a Greyhound bus alone from Florida to Michigan. He had not played the event prior. When he checked into the tournament, an older player, competing in the 18s, grabbed his bag, walked him to his room, and said, "Hey, if you need anything, my name is Vitas." Of course, my friend knew who he was. Vitas Gerulaitis is a Hall of Fame player and person. John Rast eventually played for Stanford on the same team as John McEnroe.

John Rast: I was fifteen. I had just come from National Clay Courts in Louisville where I lost a 5-4 tiebreaker in the semis. I was distraught. The next stop on the junior circuit was the Western in Springfield, Ohio. I had no transportation so I took a bus (after he had already taken a bus by himself from St. Petersburg, FL to Louisville). Everybody had left. I took a bus from Louisville to Springfield. I got to Springfield at 9 pm. I got to the dorm at the university with two bags of soaking wet clothes that I hadn't washed from the previous week, and my suitcase and tennis bag. I got to the dorm and dropped a bunch of stuff on the floor. I heard a voice, ...'Let me get that for you. Let me help you...' We continued to walk to the elevator bay. 'No, I'll take you to your room.' We got to my dorm room, we put my stuff down. He put his hand out, 'My name is Vitas. I'm here to help you. I'll do anything I can to make your week very nice. If you need something, tell anybody, "I need to see Vitas.' I'll come help you.' That was something. I didn't see him again until Kalamazoo. The draws are up. I see his name in the 18s as no. 1 seed. I didn't know who he was, he didn't tell me who he was. Oh my God, he was no. 1 in the world, no. 1 in America. Two years later he was killing it. Phenomenal career.

About six years later - I'm from St. Petersburg, FL - I was at Hopman training. Vitas was there too, training to get used to the heat before the US Open. I stopped to get a sandwich in line. I hear this voice behind me, 'John, how are you? I turned around. Six years later. It was Vitas. He said, 'It's good to see you...' He was such a gentleman. He helped me with laundry, buy food, so warm, so nice. Never forgot it. He was such a kind human. That was our relationship. He had no motive or anything. It was just an act of kindness. I was going to Stanford when John McEnroe was there. I played with Bill Scanlon, Sandy Mayer, Saviano, Tim Mayotte, Peter Rennert, and nobody was like Vitas was. None of them ever did anything like what Vitas did. He didn't tell me who he was, which was incredible. I'll never forget it.

Bill Koegler: I was very close friends with Vitas at the time of his death. Incredibly sad. Vitas and I had some wild times together, and he and I had many things planned for the future. I collect cars, and he sometimes would drive one around for a few days when he was in Los Angeles, and he had a key to my condo in Brentwood, near Barrington and San Vicente, between Sunset and San Vicente. He and I and Wilt Chamberlain played three times at the Barrington courts and at The Riviera Tennis Club, where I was a member. Then they were gone... passed away, my heart aches still.

Brad Gilbert: Funniest player I ever saw in my life, bar none, the guy could tell the best locker room stories out of anybody I ever met in my whole life Vitas Gerulaitis.

Head to head series tied 2-2

1984 Wimbledon Grass R32   Gerulaitis 7-6 6-1 3-6 6-4

1983 Tokyo Indoor   Carpet   R16   Gilbert 6-3 2-6 7-5

1983 Forest Hills WCT   Clay   Gerulaitis 7-5 7-6

1982 Sydney Indoor   Hard R32 Gilbert 6-3 6-4

Bunner Smith: Wild memories... I met him during summer national tour in 1971. We hung out more during summer of '72 when he lost at Kalamazoo in the quarters ... he was really pissed. When Nick Bollettieri sent me to Baltimore in 1981 to run his academy there, I went up to New York City a lot and we went to Butch Seewagen's bar 'Center Court' a lot late nights. Vitas was a regular there. He remembered me from juniors and other Florida players Rick Fagel and Don Petrine were good friends of mine that played with Vitas at Columbia. He was living the life ... playing great tennis and partying hard ... lot of beautiful ladies always around his table wherever he went. He had a perfect white Rolls Royce convertible that he had valet keep close at Studio and he always had a smile. He had fastest feet and hands I ever saw and a monster forehand, great volleys - maybe best ever. His serve wasn't a weapon and it probably kept him from winning a Grand Slam (correction - Vitas won Australian Open). But, he was a celebrity and all around fun guy. Sad sad thing that happened to him. He went to sleep and never woke up. But he had the good life when life was really wild in the 1080s and early 90s till he died in 1994. Tough loss for New York tennis players. He was really tight with Borg and McEnroe. Great hair!

Brian Gottfried: Although Vitas and I were close in age we didn't hang out a lot together on tour. He was single and I had a family so each of those facts took us in different directions. Having said that, Vitas always had a smile on his face for all of us, whether he hung with us or not.

On the court, his strength was definitely his speed and court coverage ability. His groundies were very solid but not punishing, but since he could cover the court so well from the baseline and also when he came in, he was extremely difficult to get the ball by. So you tried to force the ball by him, and as a result, you would make more errors. His weakness was his second serve but because of his speed he was able to compensate to some degree for that.

We tried to recruit him at Trinity University in San Antonio, Texas when I was there, but he ended up turning pro right out of high school (actually Vitas attended and played one year at Columbia University in NYC).

What a sad day when he died and what tragic circumstances. He was way too young. I don't think we know the whole story.

Gerulaitis won head to head series 3-1

1977 Rome   Clay QF Gerulaitis 62 76 46 75

1978 Wimbledon   Grass QF Gerulaitis 75 46 97 62

1978 Pepsi Grand Slam Hard   Gottfried 63 63

1979 WCT Finals Hard   QF Gerulaitis 64 63 63

Hans Gildemeister: I played him two times and lost both times in straight sets. I remember Monte Carlo, was very very windy, when he came to the net was hard to pass him . Don't remember the match at Delray Beach. Was a good friend of him, nice guy.

Question: Do you have a lasting memory of Vitas off the court?

Hans Gildemeister: What happens in Vegas, stays in Vegas [smiles].

Gerulaitis won head to head series 2-0

1980 Monte Carlo Clay QF Gerulaitis   61 64

1985 Delray Beach Clay R64   61 62

Jan Triska: The era of McEnroe, Connors, Gerulaitis and Borg… they seemed divine, supernatural creatures, making a hard game look easy. The racquets were basic, not the high tech equipment of the "Big Three" era of men's tennis. Try playing with the gear of 1980 today and see how it goes.

Gene Mayer: I played Vitas four times and lost each time. I never won a set from him. He was very quick, it was hard to dictate points against him, he transitioned from defense to offense seamlessly.

My lasting memory of Vitas... his huge heart, incredibly generous, always upbeat, a real zest for life, a real concern for inner-city youth and how he took great care of his family.

Gerulaitis won head to head series 4-0

1980 Sydney Indoor   Hard SF Gerulaitis   6-4 6-3

1979 Forest Hills WCT   Clay   RR Gerulaitis 6-1 6-2

1977 Wimbledon Grass R64 Gerulaitis 6-3 6-1 6-1

1975 Roanoke   Carpet   R16   Gerulaitis   6-2 6-3

Ed Wolfarth: In the late 70s I was one of his hitting partners at Alley Pond Tennis in Queens, where his dad, Vitas Sr, was tennis director. In the early 80s, Vitas often went to Turnberry Isles in Miami to hit and train with Fred Stolle. He had a great work ethic. One rainy day he took all the kids who were watching him train, bowling in his Rolls Royce! One of them was my daughter. He was a pied piper. Loved by all.

Fred Stolle: I was coaching Vitas when he beat 'Willy' in that monumental 1979 Italian Open final 67 76 67 64 62. It finished late and a good friend of the players flew the group to Paris for start of the French Open. All good friends enjoying each other's company. An enjoyable experience from the 'good old days.'

I started coaching Vitas in New York (1977-1983). It was probably the best three or four years that I had in tennis. Very enjoyable. Wonderful guy. He left us far too early. He had a great career. He was very, very good. He was a pleasure to work with as a player and also as a TV broadcaster. After tennis, he was addicted to golf. He had to play everywhere he went. He played 18 holes of golf every day. He was very superstitious as well. Traveling around Europe. He'd say, 'Fred, let's go to this restaurant.' If he won the match, we had to go back there the next day. We went to the famous duck restaurant in Paris (Caneton Tour d'Argent). We were there, Vitas never drank. He ordered a Coca Cola. The waiter said, 'We don't serve Coca Cola.' So he had to drink orange juice. I think he drank all their orange juice [smiles].

His parents were very, very special people. We'd practice at his home in New York. Bjorn Borg was there. His mom would make lunch for us, do all the laundry, just a wonderful woman.

My first memory of Vitas is I saw him play. When he came to New York, Broadway Vitas with the yellow Rolls Royce going for him. He was recognized by everyone. I watched him play. He was very, very quick. Probably one of the quickest movers to ever play. Him and Johan Kriek were two of the fastest guys around, even today. My favorite Vitas matches... a couple. One was when I was coaching him and doing TV for Channel 9 Australia. He got to the finals of the Masters in New York against Ivan Lendl. We always had a plan of attack against Ivan. I was always a proponent for hitting the backhand return down the line, hit the chip return down the line and cover the line. In that match Vitas had match point. On second serve he chipped the return and went in and covered the line. Vitas went in two steps forward and then stopped and took one step back. And then he lost the match 75 in the fifth set. After the match he knew exactly what he did wrong.

The second, he beat Jimmy Connors at French Open that particular year (1980 semifinals 61 36 76 62 64). They played a really close match and Vitas edged it. Our policy was to serve to Jimmy's forehand on big points. I believed in serving to the lefty's forehand on the big points in the deuce court. Most players serve wide the lefty's backhand, that's what everybody sits on waiting for. Nadal's serve down the middle to the ad court against Federer was his go-to serve for many years. Vitas was very, very good to coach. He would listen. He understood I was there to try to help him and not take advantage.

John Cavanaugh: Vitas was the man. The writers would ask the players where they were going at night after the Open and they said, "Wherever Vitas is going." Borg stayed with Vitas at his home on the Island with its own court. My dad Jack Cavanaugh covered the Open from Forest Hills to Flushing and always said the writers loved him. I was lucky enough to meet him back then. Broke my heart when he died. Took the wrong guy. One of the biggest gut punches I can ever remember in sports. Everyone shed a tear for Vitas. A true legend the likes of who we'll never see again.

Lisa Kerkorian: I first met Vitas Gerulaitis at the US Open in 1981. I was coming into the player lounge as he was leaving. I was starstruck – I wasn't yet sixteen and here was a legend of the game, a man larger than life with an energy about him: charismatic and cool. My lasting memory, though, is of him as person. Jovial, fun to be around, always kind and generous with his time. I got to know him well in 1984, when eight of us went on an exhibition tour of Japan. He was wearing Maggia at the time, and I recall thinking how stylish he looked – and how my clothes felt second rate in comparison.

Kyle Johnson: I got to play doubles twice against Vitas on the Satellite circuit in San Antonio and North Carolina after I finished playing at Penn State. It was mid to late 70s. Players like Vitas, Connors, Nastase would sometimes play Satellites to stay sharp between the bigger tournaments. I remember Vitas hit with a lot of top spin, if you didn't get in the right position to hit his ball it would bounce right over you. And he was just so friendly, so nice. Not like the other guys like Nastase and eh...

Rob Glickman: A lot of people don't know who Vitas really was. Everybody thinks he was a cocaine addicted tennis pro. He worked very hard to get to no. 4 in the world, he trained very hard. He liked to party and date beautiful models like Carol Alt and Janet Jones. Vitas Sr. was my boss. Ruta was a year younger than me, I was two years younger than Vitas. Ruta was the most beautiful girl in the world. I had the biggest crush on her. One day at

Port Washington I was playing with Larry Davidson, an excellent player, and on the court next to us was Vitas and John McEnroe playing a challenge match. While I was playing Larry, I was also watching them play at the same time [smiles]. Seven years later they were both in the US Open final. When Vitas was in 12th grade, McEnroe was in seventh or eighth grade. I trained with Vitas, two hours of drills, Harry Hopman had us doing everything. When we were all at Port Washington, you're not exactly friends, more like competitors. Vitas was an amazing athlete, he could have been professional soccer player or baseball player. He could have chosen any sport but he picked tennis. McEnroe also played soccer and basketball in high school and he chose to concentrate on tennis.

A lasting memory of Vitas? Probably going to Studio 54 and seeing Vitas there on the dance floor with two beautiful models. The confidence he had wherever he went. He was handsome, blond, confident and generous. He was my idol. Everybody wanted to be Vitas. Did you know he put white gauze tape on his grip? He learned that from me. I think about him almost every day. I wonder what he'd be like as a 60 year old. Like he was becoming a good TV analyst and interviewer. It's too bad he passed away too young. Everybody loves Vitas, Pete Sampras, McEnroe, Connors, Borg. Did you see who came to his funeral? It's great that you are doing a book about Vitas. I hope they make it into a movie.

Bjorn Borg: Vitas Gerulaitis meant a lot to me, and Jimmy too, he was a great friend, like a brother to me. I knew him longer and better than anybody and I feel like I've lost a member of my family. We played semifinals of Wimbledon 1977. We had a great match. I was lucky to win 8-6 in the fifth set. I was practicing the next day at Hurlingham, a club outside London. After one hour of practice, who's coming? Vitas. He came up to me and said, 'Good match.' I would never do that (compliment an opponent the next day after such an important loss). So he came up, we practiced together, after that we were spending so much time together. He did so much for tennis, charities, he was the first to start a charity. He was a great person, great friend, huge heart, I miss him a lot. He could joke, be serious. If he would be here today, he'd be in the TV commentator box... He's not in the Hall of Fame? If he doesn't get in the Hall of Fame, I'm ready to drop out.

I remember the day of the Roland Garros semifinals in 1980, and I was in the locker room waiting to enter the court to play against Solomon. The match before that was between Connors and Gerulaitis. Vitas won 6-4 in the fifth, came into the locker room and the first thing he did was come up to me, hug me and say, 'You're lucky, you're going to play me in the final and not Jimmy. Then I beat Solomon (6-2 6-2 6-0) and the next day, as we were close friends, Vitas and I had dinner together and he said to me, laughing, 'Hey, you're going to have a tough match tomorrow!' He was very happy to have beaten Jimmy and to have reached the French Open final. (Borg won the final 6-4 6-1 6-2.)

Borg won head to head series 17-0

1981 Wimbledon Grass R16   Borg 7-6 7-5 7-6

1980 Roland Garros   Clay   F   Borg 6-4 6-1 6-2

1980 Las Vegas   Hard SF   Borg 6-4 3-6 6-2

1980 Monte Carlo Clay SF   Borg 6-0 6-2

1980 Pepsi Grand Slam Clay F Borg   6-1 5-7 6-1

1980 Masters   Carpet   F   Borg 6-2 6-2

1979 Roland Garros   Clay SF Borg   6-2 6-1 6-0

1979 Dallas WCT Carpet   SF Borg   7-5 7-6 2-6 6-2

1979 Monte Carlo Clay F Borg   6-2 6-1 6-3

1978 Davis Cup WG   Carpet   SF Borg   6-3 6-1

1978	US Open	Hard	SF	Borg (1)	6-3 6-2 7-6
1978	Dallas WCT	Carpet	SF	Gerulaitis	W/O
1978	Milan WCT	Carpet	F	Borg	6-3 6-3
1978	Las Vegas	Carpet	F	Borg	6-5 5-6 6-4 6-5
1978	Birmingham WCT	Carpet	SF	Borg	6-4 7-6
1977	Wimbledon	Grass	SF	Borg	6-4 3-6 6-3 3-6 8-6
1976	Toronto Indoor WCT	Carpet	F	Borg	2-6 6-3 6-1
1974	Tehran	Clay	R16	Borg	3-6 6-2 6-2

Jimmy Connors: Vitas was seventeen and I was nineteen when we first met, after he joined the Bill Riordan circuit. We hung out a lot together in the 70s and 80s. When I won the US Open in 1978, I went out for a celebration dinner at Maxwell's Plum in Manhattan. Vitas drove up and parked right in front of the restaurant. And let me tell you, he was hard to miss. He drove a yellow Rolls Royce. He got out of the car with two cute young girls who couldn't have been a day over eighteen, waltzed in and sat down and congratulated me. He was the only one who did that. He was all class. What the public saw was the real Vitas - the dazzling smile, the free-spirited guitar playing rocker, the playboy lifestyle - yet he was one of the most decent guys I've ever known and everybody liked him.

Vitas brought a lot to tennis. Not just his athletic style of play but also his rock star sex appeal, which added a new dimension to the Tour. He was wild and flamboyant but also a great champion, winning the Australian Open in 1977 (defeated Lloyd 63 76 57 36 62) and reaching the finals of the French Open (1980 vs Borg) and US Open (1979 vs McEnroe). He was a Davis Cup participant and winner of 25 Grand Prix tournaments. Is any of that recognized by tennis establishment? No. Vitas had a Hall of Fame career but apparently he didn't have a Hall of Virtue career - but who does? It's a joke he's not in the Hall of Fame. If he doesn't get in maybe we (Connors and his pal Bjorn Borg) should drop out.

I don't know how you want to remember Vitas. You tend to go only to the good and that's not fair. I think it's more interesting and intriguing to remember it all. I think I miss the good, the bad and ugly of it all - that makes one become a friend.

(Excerpts from "The Outsider Jimmy Connors A Memoir" Published by Harper.)

Connors won head to head series 19-5

1985 Montreal / Toronto   Hard R16 Connors 6-4 6-2

1983 Wembley   Carpet   QF   Connors 6-4 6-2

1982 Montreal / Toronto   Hard SF Gerulaitis W/O

1982 Brussels   Hard SF Gerulaitis   6-2 7-5

1981 Cincinnati   Hard R16   Gerulaitis   7-5 7-6

1980 Roland Garros   Clay SF   Gerulaitis   6-1 3-6 6-7 6-2 6-4

1980 Masters   Carpet   SF   Gerulaitis   7-5 6-2

1979 Tokyo Indoor   Carpet   SF   Connors 6-7 6-2 6-3

1979 Memphis   Carpet   SF   Connors   3-6 6-3 6-2

1979 Dorado Beach   Hard F   Connors   6-5 6-0 6-4

1979 Dorado Beach   Hard RR   Connors 6-0 6-4

1979 Birmingham Carpet   SF   Connors   7-6 6-2

1978 Wimbledon Grass SF   Connors   9-7 6-2 6-1

1978 Rotterdam WTC   Carpet   SF   Connors   4-6 6-4 6-4

1978 Pepsi Grand Slam   Clay   SF   Connors   6-2 6-4

1976 Las Vegas   Carpet   SF   Connors   5-7 7-6 7-6 6-1

1976 WCT Challenge Cup   Hard SF   Connors   5-7 7-6 7-6 6-1

1976 Las Vegas   Carpet   RR   Connors   6-4 6-4

1976 US Open   Clay   R16   Connors   6-4 6-3 6-1

1975 Bermuda   Clay   F   Connors   6-1 6-4

1975 New York   Hard (i)   F   Gerulaitis   W/O

1975 Salisbury   Carpet   F   Connors   5-7 7-5 6-1 3-6 6-0

1974 Salt Lake City   Hard (i)   F Connors   4-6 7-6 6-3

1974 Little Rock   Carpet   SF   Connors d. Gerulaitis   6-2 6-1

1974	Roanoke	Carpet	SF	Connors	6-4 6-4	
1972	New York	Carpet	R32	Gerulaitis	6-4 4-6 6-3	

Joy DeVijon: I love Vitas, but cocaine did him in. I watched him play outside of Venice in December 1984. 30 years old. He was a sluggish shadow of his former self. I think he managed to right himself before his sad end. Generous soul. He took me to dinner in 1978, where he introduced me to Reggie Jackson! Then to "Studio" - he never said "54" or "Studio 54". McEnroe and Fleming were there looking lost. I got a ride home in his yellow Rolls. Well, actually, he dropped me off at the entrance to the Midtown Tunnel. It happened a few times. I'm still talking about!

Question: Vitas was tight with Reggie Jackson too?

Joy DeVijon: I can't say. But, we were having dinner, at Mortimer's, I think, and Vitas saw Reggie at a table for two. I think Reggie was alone, maybe not. Vitas took me over and we were introduced. I don't remember speaking to anyone else at Reggie's table. I think Vitas and Reggie knew each other. Vitas hadn't been famous for long, so it wasn't an old friendship. Stars colliding. Everyone loved Vitas. He introduced me to Steve Rubell, but I wasn't interested in Studio, so I never made use of the connection. I only went with Vitas. I invited Dustin Hoffman there once, but he didn't need me to get in!

Question: You name dropper you! Why did Vitas drop you off at the Midtown Tunnel entrance?

Joy DeVijon: Every pro in New York City knew Vitas and Dustin, and many more. Tennis was hot then. Vitas was going through the tunnel to the LIE, going home to King's Point. I didn't want to take him out of his way so I took the cab home.

Question: Where did you first meet Vitas?

Joy DeVijon: A Ford fashion model introduced us.

Question: One more Vitas memory please?

Joy DeVijon: I heard that when his high school soccer team from Archbishop Molloy played in Yankee Stadium it was Vitas who scored the only goal...Of course. I heard he scored the only goal. He rose to the moment. I don't know whether it was the only goal in the game or the only one scored by his team.

Ken Williams: Met Vitas walking the grounds at 1991 US Open he said hi to me and my friend, we shook hands. He was such a down to earth person. I remember the Sergio Tacchini, yellow and white outfit he wore in the 1979 US Open. My first US Open that I attended in 1983, the 16 year old Aaron Krickstein upset Gerulaitis in five sets. Also saw McEnore lose to the late Bill Scanlon, this was on Labor Day Weekend. It was a bummer watching my two favorite players lose that weekend.

Glenn Muller: He was a ladies man for sure. But men loved him too. Vitas was a very cool guy and great player and a giant personality that lives on.

The great Vitas. What a great guy and spirit. He hit with me as a kid for an hour, when I was twelve, after bringing him his lunch, the lunch he ordered and forgot about. We hit in Panama City, FL. And years later I got to work for him at Lavers Club in Delray Beach Florida.

Carl Vaughn: I watched Vitas play against McEnroe in my hometown, Springfield, MO, when they were touring the US during McEnroe's "Tennis Over America" in 1983. Great match! McEnroe won of course. There was a capacity crowd of 10,000 indoors, at the Missouri State University basketball arena called Hammon's Student Center. McEnroe played to the crowd with his typical rants at refs, etc., which really drew the applause from the spectators. That's what they wanted and came there to see. Very good pro tennis skills displayed by both players. In the first match that night, McEnroe played a set against the top player on the university tennis team and gave him a free clinic.

Jonathan Chimene: Vitas didn't win more Grand Slams because his head to head record against Borg, McEnroe and Connors was 8-46. That's eight more wins than you and I had against these all-time greats that Vitas competed with. Vitas was great, but he had the misfortune of playing against three absolute legends. Andy Roddick suffered a similar fate, in my opinion.

Timothy Vann: I played Vitas twice, was up there in New York for the 1979 US Open. I called him to get in the Studio 54, No luck. Cheryl Tiegs was in the crowd looking down fondly.

Question: Your memories of playing Vitas twice?

Timothy Vann: Beat him in doubles with George Hardie as my partner, he had Henry Bunis. Lost in 1976 on the Bill Riordan circuit, where I came with no jock or underwear. As I trained, strung rackets - Jimmy Connors still owes me for five T-2000 jobs, and umpired with Frank Hammond. With no undies I grabbed the tallest ball boy and used his underwear, losing to Vitas 2 and 4. Parties every night. Ilie Nastase and Tom Okker ran after all the junior league women.

Lee Morris: I was fortunate to meet Borg and Vitas at the California Club 1978, North Miami Beach directed by Gardnar Mulloy, who previously directed the famous Fountainbleau Hotel courts. My doubles partner Joe Nazzarro and I played highly ranked Florida mens doubles so we were fortunate to play a set against Borg and Gardnar's assistant.

Jeffrey Scott: I remember Borg and Vitas bumping me off the court at Glen Cove. We did get to sit on the sideline and watch though.

Question: Any standout memories?

Jeffrey Scott: When Vitas got on the court, Borg was still getting his shoes and I jumped on the other side and I asked to hit with him and he wouldn't. He said, 'If I hit with you, I have to hit with everybody.'

Gregory Nimensky: Vitas gave me my first lesson in Delray Beach, FL. Twelve years later I was on the Columbia men's tennis team.

Question: Remember any specifics?

Gregory Nimensky: Just that I thought he was the coolest guy ever with the coolest hair ever and that I wanted to learn how to play tennis because of him.

Luigi Stasi: Borg and Vitas both practiced together at Cumberland grass courts NW3, London every year, the week before and during Wimbledon. I was at the time working nearby and always spent my lunch breaks among a few club members watching them train.

John Lloyd: Vitas was a player in the shadows of the greatest, Borg, Connors, McEnroe. No one has contributed more than him to make of tennis the coolest sport of its generation. We called him 'Broadway Vitas. It was interesting hanging out with him, though I didn't have the stamina to do that for very long, given what he used to get up to. You never picked up a tab with Vitas. It didn't matter if you went out with him and ten other people he didn't even know. He had his credit card out before anybody. Someone told me one year, he had the third highest American Express bill for an individual in the world. I went with him to Studio 54 a couple times. There were queues for blocks outside, but he would just walk straight in because everybody knew him.

He would party hard, but he would do it during periods when he was taking a break from the tennis circuit. He would punish himself by training hard for a month, practicing eight hours a day. He was one of the fittest guys and it was weird really to think that he did all the other stuff. His work ethic when he wasn't partying was beyond belief. During tournaments he would never drink. When he was playing he wouldn't do the other stuff either. His idea of partying would be to go out with girls.

Question: You played Vitas in the 1977 Australian Open final and also had breakfast with him that morning and you also practiced together?

John Lloyd: I remember being worried about practicing again. So I asked, 'Should we practice together?' He responded by saying, 'What can I f------ learn about your game? And what more can you learn about my game? Of course, we'll practice together!'

Gerulaitis won head to head series 3-2

1983 Sydney Outdoor   Grass R64   John Lloyd   7-5 6-3

1979 South Orange   Clay SF   John Lloyd   6-4 1-6 6-4

1977 Australian Open-2 Grass F   Gerulaitis 6-3 7-6 5-7 3-6 6-2

1977 Sydney Outdoor   Grass R32   Gerulaitis 6-2 6-2

1974 Barcelona   Clay   R32   Gerulaitis 3-6 7-5 7-5

Ruta Gerulaitis: He was very family-oriented and understood the sacrifices our parents made. I was the luckiest sister on the planet having Vitas as a brother. Even from our teenage years, he dragged me along everywhere he went, so we became very close. He thought it was great we all still lived in the home that he was able to buy.

Patrick McEnroe: Vitas was very humble. He was obviously a great player, but he also knew that he wasn't as great as Connors, Borg or my brother, who were three of the greatest players ever. He had that self-deprecating style about himself. When you compared him to everyone else on the planet, 99.8 per cent of the rest of the people, he was amazing. He was an all-time player as far as a Top 5 player, but that was his demeanor. That was really the way he was.

Even with Borg, who was his best buddy, he couldn't beat Borg... And even with John, he knew John was just a better player, more talented, but Vitas seemed to be content with where he was. It wasn't like he was jealous. I'm sure there was a part of him that thought, 'I wish I had John's touch, I wish I had Borg's relentless competitiveness.' Vitas had what he had, which was pretty damn good when you consider what he did with his career.

Vitas obviously liked to live it up a little bit but he was also a guy who was a very hard worker and extremely fit. In a way his lifestyle with the fancy cars and going to the night clubs [wasn't like his tennis]. The way he played was more about bringing your hard hat to the court. He was just a grinder, he wasn't a flashy player. But he was tremendously consistent and tremendously quick and very, very fit. Really, if you look at the way he lived his life, he was kind of a partier, and loved to have a great time, so you would think he would have been more of a risk taker in the way he played. But he really wasn't.

He worked his butt off to get really good. He wasn't a natural talent in the same way my brother was with the racquet. I think he had to really school himself and drive himself with his strokes to get really solid. It wasn't like he was a flashy player. I wouldn't call him a guy with great hands like an [Ilie] Nastase or John. He was a workhorse and that's how he became a Top 5 player.

Steve Flink: His personality and lifestyle overshadowed his greatness as a player. No doubt about that. He was a natty dresser who loved living in the jet-set. But that was only a part of who he was. He also was a top of the line professional who worked very hard at his craft and competed with a lot of integrity. But he just happened to come along in a golden era of the sport. He was haunted by not only Connors and Borg but also by McEnroe. Those three superstars were the pace setters of their era. But the great thing about Gerulaitis was his sense of humility and perspective. He fought hard against those guys on the court but was a good friend of both away from the arena. He seemed to be able to separate friendship from business. He never held grudges against those guys. Vitas was very close to McEnroe as well. McEnroe and Connors were always at odds with each other. Yet what they most had in common was their genuine respect for Gerulaitis.

Andy Warhol: "Monday August 22, 1977... Cabbed to Chembank ($3.40). Walked over to University Place to look for things to paint. Then cabbed over to Richard Weisman's with Susan Johnson. When we got there, everyone was watching the Wimbledon match between

Bjorn Borg and Vitas Gerulaitis. Those two weren't there yet, they were having dinner together. The match went on three hours, and somewhere in there Vitas came in with a girlfriend but Bjorn had gone home from dinner. The joke is always that Bjorn sleeps for four hours then plays tennis for two, and that Vitas plays tennis for two hours then discotheques for four. Now Vitas has just discovered New York/New York... There was a lot to drink, no cocaine. Everyone teased Gerulaitis that he was wearing his gold coke-cutter razorblade around his neck in the match. He's in training now, he left early and only ate a plum."
(Excerpt from "The Andy Warhol Diaries", Edited By Pat Hackett, Pan Books 1992.)

Shelby Rogers: When I played Ash Barty at US Open in 2021 I had lost to her all five times before, and four times earlier in the year. You know what's funny? That morning, I was watching the video of Vitas Gerulaitis when he said, 'Nobody beats me 17 times in a row,' ... I was only at six!' I just said, 'Make balls, try to stay in this match, it can't get any worse [because] you've lost to her every time, so try something different.'

I told myself I didn't want to lose the same way I lost the last five times against her. In the first set, I mixed in some high balls, I was super patient with her slice because she's not going to miss one very often. I know that very well. In the second and third, she definitely raised her level. I mean, she was the No. 1 player in the world for a reason. But I started wanting to hit the ball a little bit harder, find some winners if I could. That's the tennis I like to play. That's what she wants me to do. She wants to redirect and finesse me around the court, wait for me to miss. I was just happy and really proud of myself for problem-solving, if you will, maybe doing some things I'm not super comfortable with, like hitting some high balls like I'm back in the [age 12-and-under juniors], playing defense honestly. It ended up working somehow." (Rogers won 62 16 76, she was down 25 in the final set.)

Pete Sampras: I couldn't tell you I had any close friends in high school. You need them. Vitas was someone I can talk to...We'd been friends ever since he saw how I was struggling on clay, he sought me out to encourage and advise me. He had credibility because even though he played serve and volley tennis, he's won the Italian Open twice. He told me that if he could do it, he could do it too. I really respected what Vitas had achieved with his daring, chip and charge game. And he was just a great guy to be around because of his energy, big personality and obvious zest for life.

Vitas, Tim (Gullikson) and I spent a fair amount of time together in Tampa where I lived for training purposes for most of my career. Vitas would come by frequently, he was a golf nut after he quit tennis and he liked to play with Tim. Our friendship surprised many people because we were so different. Vitas, in his heyday, was the ultimate glam tennis player - a habitue of Studio 54, who had the charisma, big hair and habits of a rock star. He was a favorite of Andy Warhol and a regular in the New York gossip pages.

After I lost that match to Jaime Yzaga (in five sets at US Open 1994). I'd collapsed on the floor in the trainer's room, and there were all these doctors hovering around, and Vitas was there, after he saw the condition I was in, he rushed down from the commentary booth as soon as the last ball was hit. And I told everyone to leave but him. Vitas unlaced my shoes, put a dry shirt on me, packed up my bag, and told me he understood just how bad I was feeling. He was just there to get me better, and that's the memory I have of him. That's the sort of friend he was. I didn't know it at the time but that was the last I would see of my friend Vitas. I think we would have been friends forever. (Excerpt from "Pete Sampras: A Champion's Mind" Crown Publishers Random House.)

Tim Mayotte: He won by being wily and being quick. I don't buy the implications that he wasted his talent, or didn't develop it to the fullest, because he got involved in drugs. I don't think he ever shortchanged himself on the tennis court. He had no big weapons, and for him to achieve what he did in an era that put him up against the likes of Borg, McEnroe and Connors, I really think Vitas maxed out the talent he had.

Head to head series tied 1-1

1985 Tokyo Indoor   Carpet   R32 Mayotte 6-2 6-1

1982 Brussels   Hard QF Gerulaitis   6-3 6-4

John McEnroe: It was an incredible moment for both of us to play the US Open final. Two kids from Queens, fifteen minutes from Flushing Meadows... Everything that I'm involved in and enjoy, whether it's music, art, commentating, has something to do with him.

What I always remember first about Vitas is his hair, long and blond like Borg's, only Vitas never wore a headband. He was clearly imitating Borg but I never thought any less of him for that. Because, first, it was a cool look if you could bring it off and, second, Vitas was a much stronger personality. People mistook him for Borg all the time but he kind of got a kick out of it. It certainly never hurt his social life. I first became aware of Vitas after I first started playing at Port Washington. I would stand in the lounge and gaze down at the courts, watching him run around with those little bunny hop steps of his. Harry Hopman always spoke admiringly about Vitas's work ethic and it was true. He was always practicing and he could run all day.

There were a lot of strong players at Port Washington but in terms of drive, talent, and charisma, Vitas was clearly the star. Even early on when people used to joke - 'Vitas Gerulaitis, what is that, a disease?' - it looked as though he was going to be tremendously famous. I adored him like crazy. But he wouldn't give me the time of day when I was fourteen or fifteen. And why should he? He was already Broadway Vitas, going out with the likes of Cheryl Tiegs. Why should he pay attention to some fifteen year old? He brushed me off which only made him seem more magnetic.

I first made it into Vitas's radar screen when I was

seventeen and we played a charity match at the Felt Forum in Madison Square Garden. The match was one of those bouts between the up-and-comer and the established superstar. There were no upsets that night. The superstar won. But at least Vitas would speak to me now.

By early 1979 quite a bit had changed. I'd won the Masters. I was number four in the world to Vitas's number three, behind Borg and Connors, two players he would never surpass. I was no longer the blip on the screen, I was the jet coming up fast behind them. Vitas never beat Borg in a big match. I think Vitas figured he could live with that. Borg was just colossally great, and he was near-great. I think that if anyone really frustrated Vitas, it was me.

Vitas had a great run at the 1979 US Open. He beat Jose-Luis Clerc in the round of sixteen, Johan Kriek in the quarterfinals, Roscoe Tanner in the semis, Tanner had just gotten revenge on Borg for his five set Wimbledon loss. It was funny how Vitas could beat guys who had beaten Borg and yet, when it came down to it, he couldn't handle Borg himself. Tennis always works that way. Then in the finals Vitas faced me.

I was coming off a year in which I had won three big victories over Connors - in the Masters, at Dallas, where I'd beaten Borg to win the tournament, and now here at the Open, in straight sets in the semis. I felt it was my time. I was a little uncomfortable about having to play my buddy Vitas in a big match, but not uncomfortable enough to lose.

It wasn't even a particularly close match. I won in straight sets 75 63 63. I think Vitas was more uncomfortable than I was. People were booing because they were angry that Connors and Borg weren't playing. At that moment, they were the real stars, we were just two guys from Queens.

For a couple of years, I'd been working to hang out with Vitas, wondering if I could keep up with him off the court. I'd been trying to be his friend. I looked up to him. And now that I had blown him away, the victory felt hollow. I had taken something from him. He was still a legitimate no. 4 in the world but now he was off the mountaintop. Now it was Borg, Connors and me. Things were never quite the same between Vitas and me after that.

At the 1991 US Open, a couple of rounds after the match where Michael Chang topspin-lobbed me to death, I stopped by the USA Network broadcast booth to visit my buddy Vitas, who had begun a promising new career as a tennis commentator. At the time, I'd thought Vitas was head and shoulders above almost any of the broadcasters out there, which wasn't saying a lot, since I felt, and still feel that most of them stank. Virtually without exception, they were arrogant, dry, pompous or just plain boring, take your pick.

Jimmy Connors was playing Paul Haarhuis in a quarterfinal that night and though Jimmy had been wildcarded into the tournament at the astounding age of 39, he was giving Haarhuis one hell of a match. Vitas was giving commentary along with Ted Robinson and not knowing enough about commentating to be afraid, I fell into a natural give-and-take with the two of them. At one point in the match Jimmy started throwing up lobs at Haarhuis, who kept hitting smashes. And Jimmy kept running each one down and throwing up another lob. This happened several times in a row until Jimmy ended the point with an incredible running winner which drove the Flushing Meadows crowd into a frenzy. That was the greatest point I ever saw at the US Open.

(In 1994) I had to fly to San Francisco to play an exhibition with Michael Chang for Michael's Bay-area charity. When I got to the auditorium, Michael told me the event was sold out... I felt euphoric as I stood in the locker room putting on my tennis clothes, I couldn't stop thinking about Patty (Smyth), my luck was finally changing. Then someone walked in and told me Vitas had died. I was staggered. Vitas had just turned 40 in July. He was still a young man. I had worried about him for a long time but lately he seemed to have turned his life around. He was taking better care of himself.

I walked on the court numb. Was I going to play tennis? Apparently, I was. I started to hit with Michael, just going through the motions I'd gone through a million times before - forehands, backhands, volleys, overheads. "Mr. McEnroe has won the toss. He has elected to serve." I served still numb. Ace. Fifteen-love. I served again. Numb. Thirty-love. Two more points. "Game, Mr. McEnroe. He leads one game to love."

I simply couldn't miss. I can't explain it. I couldn't miss anything. The tension of what I had come to do had totally evaporated. Nothing mattered anymore. I could see the odd look on Michael's face. He was trying as hard as he could but there was nothing he could do against me. I won the first set 64 and then the match was over 64 63. I had destroyed Michael Chang, no. 5 in the world. I'd cleaned his clock.

I pulled out of the Mexico City exhibition and stayed close by Patty's side until I flew back east to Vitas's funeral on Long Island. It was a long day that went by in a blur of tears. Jimmy Connors, Mary Carillo and Vitas's sister Ruta all gave touching tributes to Vitas but at the moment when I might have gone up and said a few words myself, I found myself too undone to move. I've regretted it ever since.

(From the 2002 book "John McEnroe: You Cannot Be Serious" with James Kaplan. G.P. Putnam's Sons Publisher.)

McEnroe won head to head series 11-3

1984 Montreal/Toronto Hard F McEnroe   60 63

1984 Dallas WCT Carpet   QF McEnroe   6-3 6-1 6-3

1984 Richmond WCT   Carpet   SF McEnroe   6-7 6-3 6-1

1983 Forest Hills WCT Clay   F   McEnroe   6-3 7-5

1983 Dallas WCT Carpet   SF McEnroe   6-3 6-2 6-2

1982 Philadelphia Carpet   SF McEnroe   6-1 6-2 6-4

1981 US Open   Hard SF   McEnroe 5-7 6-3 6-2 4-6 6-3

1980 Sydney Indoor   Hard F   McEnroe 6-3 6-4

1980 Forest Hills WCT Clay   F   Gerulaitis   2-6 6-2 6-0

1980 Pepsi Grand Slam Clay   SF   Gerulaitis   7-6 6-3

1980 Masters   Carpet   RR   Gerulaitis 3-6 7-6 7-6

1979 US Open   Hard F   McEnroe 7-5 6-3 6-3

1979 Montreal / Toronto Hard SF McEnroe 6-3 6-3

1979 Milan Carpet   SF McEnroe 6-0 6-3

Additional Vitas anecdote: I played an exhibition in Germany with Borg, Connors and Vitas. I played Connors and then Borg played Vitas. And you know, Borg never showed any emotion. They played a long rally which Vitas won and Borg said, under his breath, you could hear a pin drop there, he said, 'Shit.' Vitas got down on his knees and looked up to the sky. The crowd gave him a standing ovation. Because he showed some kind of emotion.

Steve Tignor: One of the nuggets I took from the book on Pistol Pete, by Steve Flink, called Pete Sampras: Greatness Revisited... Flink reminded us, Sampras actually won the biggest clay court title of his career at the Foro Italico, in 1994. Coached by another American player who had won the Italian Open - Vitas Gerulaitis, Sampras rolled over Boris Becker in the final that year. Unfortunately, as we know, Pete could never repeat that performance in Paris.

Bob Lutz: I admit I wasn't a big fan of Vitas early on. You know, Californians and New Yorkers don't mix well. But in the senior 35s I got to know him better and I thoroughly enjoyed his company. He had just picked up golf and went golf crazy. He was playing every day. And in every city he was taking a lesson from a different pro. I said, 'Vitas, that may not be the way to go. Every pro says it a little different and you may get totally screwed up [smiles].' I don't think he listened but he became a pretty good golfer. I remember a shot he hit at no. 2 at Pinehurst. From the rough, over a sand trap, downhill and he hit it to three feet from the hole. I clapped and said, 'Vitas, you don't know how f---ing good that was!'

Johan Kriek: In 1978 I arrived in the US to play the Satellite in Florida which was called The Watch circuit in February 1978. And I thought I was just going to play that for six weeks and go back to Austria and become a citizen, play Davis Cup for them. That was kind of my plan because my coach from South Africa emigrated so I lived with him for three years in Austria.

Anyway, by August 1978, a short few months later, I was top 200 in the world, qualified for US Open for the first time as a 20 year old and then I played with Vitas Gerulaitis in the quarterfinal. Never seen anybody play faster than me or run faster than I was... he spanked me (62 61 62). I played for the first time on center court (Louis Armstrong Stadium). So that was a big chance for me, never was in the big picture before. I won a couple of close matches before I played Gerulaitis (76 63 76 vs. Brian Teacher in fourth round, 62 67 63 vs. Rick Fagel in second round).

In 1979 a year later, I never went back to Austria, by the way, I met my first wife, got married and lived in Naples, FL. And then I played Gerulaitis again. And then when I played him the second time in 1979, I got a stadium ticket and sat as close to the bottom of it to get a better sense and feel of the size of the stadium. Because I was completely out of sync when I first played him in 1978. No wonder these guys playing earlier on the center court are the ones most used to it. If you play on a smaller court, suddenly your vision is completely changed. It's a different thing. Well, I was serving for the third set to go up two sets to one. I lost to Gerulaitis in four sets. I couldn't believe it.

So then I played him again. I had to play him in Milan, Italy in 1980. And I said to myself the night before, 'If I lose to him again, I am going to lose it.' Because he's very fast and he and I were... he was 4 in the world, I was about top 20. And I beat him badly in Milan I think (64 76), it could have been somewhere else.

I ended up playing him a lot of times (11 total). I beat him in the final of Monterrey, Mexico 1981 76 36 76 indoor carpet. Won the tournament. I had a great relationship with Vitas. The sad part of our relationship was that the weekend before he died in New York at his friend's house because of a leaky pump or something - it pumped carbon monoxide into his swimming villa. Borg and I had played him and we beat him and his partner in the semifinal of the tournament in Seattle for the Champions Tour. And that night he took a red eye back and was in New York on the Sunday morning and then went to his friend's house on the Hamptons. Then he unfortunately took a nap and then never woke up. So that was my claim to fame with Vitas, very interesting story.

Fantastic gentleman. I had a lot of fun playing with him. It was always hilarious. One time I played him and Wojtek Fibak was playing Connors in Philadelphia. And they were in the (round of 16). And the two courts were next to each other. Well, Vitas and I were running so wide for drop shots and angles that we were running into their court and disrupting their game and Connors got so pissed he sat down and said, 'I'm not playing anymore.' So Wojtek and Connors waited a half an hour watching me and Vitas play. I think I may have lost that match (64 26 57). I had so many great matches with Vitas. Some I won, some he won. But an absolute gentleman. So that's my story.

Leif Shiras: I never played him but I trained with him and know some of the good stuff [smiles]. A lot of memories come to mind. The first time we trained together was at Hopman's, he brought me there to train. It was an eye-opener how hard he could work, and play. Later we hit in Long Island and other spots, but most memorably at Hopman's. I remember Lendl pegged him in the head with a forehand at Madison Square Garden at the finals one year. Lendl could be an idiot. I think it affected how Vitas played the rest of the match, which he lost despite being ahead. The only solace for Vitas was that Lendl had to go to the hospital to get IV's after the five sets, and Vitas was out dancing at Studio.

Question: What kind of drills did Vitas like to do in practice?

Leif Shiras: Vitas was big on two-on-one drills. Two men at the net, one at the baseline who gets worked side to side. It's a real test of stamina, of building endurance, as the rally never ends and the lungs are tested. If there's a miss, a new ball is fed, so the torturous workout continues. The strongest guys could maybe go 5-6 minutes, maybe, which was a lot. Vitas would go well past that! His legs were hugely muscled and they worked relentlessly. He had a big engine and could run forever.

Not sure there is another player who got more out of their game than Vitas - and the foundation was his ability to run and play another ball -- which was the essence of the two-on-one drills.

Barry Beck: I played tennis with Vitas and John McEnroe, in a private match across the river in Queens. Vitas and John used to come to a lot of Rangers games. We ran in the same circles. We were all friends. I remember Vitas had extraordinary athletic ability. And hair like (teammate) Ron Duguay. We had a mutual friend who was also good friends with McEnroe - Richard Weisman. He lived in the UN Plaza, in Johnny Carson's old pad, two floors. He had some great parties there... The Stones, Cher, Bianca Jagger, Cheryl Tiegs, Jacqueline Bissett, Andy Warhol, always with a camera around his neck, LeRoy Neiman, Catherine Guinness, Bjorn Borg, Liza Minnelli. Vitas was just a good guy, a New Yorker like McEnroe. I met Truman Capote. He lived in the UN Plaza also. Richard was the link between all of us.

Andres Gomez: My first memory of Vitas was when Mr.

Hopman was in Port Washington, he had all the good players there at his academy. Then he moved to Florida and Vitas came to train in Florida, even John McEnroe and Bjorn Borg came to train. Beginning the in the early 90s Bardmoor was the place to be. A lot of players trained there, good juniors and college players and good social players. It was a very fun environment. With 45 courts it was the place to be. The first time I played with Vitas was in 1978 or even 1977. I remember practicing with Vitas when I was only seventeen (1977) and he was already three or four in the world. It was a great experience, he was such a nice guy all the time. After practice he would take us to lunch.

Question: What made him a special player?

Andres Gomez: He was a special person. All the charisma outside the courts combined with what he had inside the court, being so fast, an all attacking player, he made it special for people to come and watch. He was most of the time in a good mood.

Question: Do you have a lasting memory of Vitas?

Andres Gomez: Yeah, of course. We played a few times on the Tour. We played a lot of exhibitions also the senior tour. A tennis friendship for something like twenty years, 1977-1997. The funny thing is he came, about in 1977, for an exhibition, him, Nastase, Panatta, Ashe. He was supposed to play Panatta but Panatta was sick. So they brought me on the court - I was seventeen - 'Andres, get on the court with Vitas and he'll give you a few games...' And he beat me in a pro set 8-3. Then a year and a half later I played him on the regular Tour and I beat him (1979 in Quito R16 64 76)! Then I lost to him in Spain (Madrid QF 1984 60 67 67).

Question: You had good results vs Vitas...

Andres Gomez: Yeah, tennis was beginning to change. From smaller head racquets to mid-size. The shots on the ground became more aggressive. I was that kind of player. Vitas stuck to serve and volley. It was a change in the sport. Passing shots were able to beat the old style of game. Groundstrokes became a bigger kind of game.

Question: What was your favorite match with Vitas?

Andres Gomez: I guess at US Open (1984 R16 64 76 61). Because… New York, Grand Slam. But we had a good match in South Africa (1982 SF won by Vitas 36 61 64).

Gomez won head to head series 3-2

1984 Wembley Indoor Carpet QF Gomez 63 76

1984 US Open Outdoor Hard R16 Gomez 64 76 61

1984 Madrid Indoor Carpet QF Gerulaitis 06 76 76

1982 Johannesburg Outdoor Hard SF Gerulaitis 36 61 64

1979 Quito Outdoor Clay R16 Gomez 64 76

Fritz Buehning: I can't really share any lasting memories. Nothing you can print. Sorry. He did beat me 1, 2 and 1 in the second round at the French in 1980 on Chatrier center court. That was not fun for me [laughs]. Later I beat him at the US Open center court first round when he was the fifth seed (Armstrong Stadium 1982 64 76 63) and at Forest Hills on clay at Westside Tennis Club (1981 75 75).

Question: I read Vitas said the US Open loss to you was his

worst in a Grand Slam, what were your winning tactics?

Fritz Buehning: Aggressive on his second serve and I attacked his backhand. That was also the week he was set up by the cops for a drug buy in the city.

Question: Did you ever beat a higher seed in a Grand Slam other than Vitas the five seed at US Open?

Fritz Buehning: Nope.

Gerulaitis won head to head series 5-2

1983 US Open Hard R64 Gerulaitis 3-6 6-1 7-6 6-2

1982 US Open Hard R128 Buehning 6-4 7-6 6-3

1981 Forest Hills WCT Clay R32 Buehning 7-5 7-5

1981 Las Vegas Hard R16 Gerulaitis 7-6 7-5

1980 Melbourne Indoor Carpet SF Gerulaitis 6-4 7-5

1980 Queen's Club Grass R16 Gerulaitis 6-4 2-6 6-4

1980 Roland Garros Clay R64 Gerulaitis 6-1 6-2 6-1

Fred Mullane: Glad you are doing a book about Vitas. He should be in the Hall of Fame. I grew up with that group and spent a lot of time with him at the house and around the Carillo's also. I grew up ten minutes from Peter Fleming. Vitas achieved more than Michael Chang if you add up all his highlights beyond the Australian Open win. One of my favorite memories was, while playing for the Pittsburgh Triangles in World Team Tennis, he rented a bus for his fans, called the G Men, and drove with them to an away match in Cleveland. On the way back home, we stopped so they could play touch football. He was fast as heck.

He's also the ONLY player of his level that I can ever remember who acknowledged the other player's good shot by saying that. Not sometimes, but every single time. Ask the boys, they will tell you the same thing. Just a decent guy from day one. Never judgmental, never with an agenda, just a guy who loved his job, his mates, and life. His folks and Ruta were the same way.

If you went to the house, you could be chatting with his mother, turn around for a second, and then turn back and cakes and pies would materialize out of nowhere. I used to call her Magic Mama, because it was totally like magic.

Ilie Nastase: I'd last seen Vitas at the US Open. I was playing the seniors event. When I was in New York, I'd always practice with Vitas on an indoor court in a club. That was not easy in New York but he knew the owner. A couple of days before the end of the tournament, I noticed he has this little phone with an earpiece. And I asked him where he got the phone because I wanted to buy one as well. I asked him how much it was? He said, 'I don't know, $300 or something, Come on let's go, I'll take you there.' So we went to this store and in typical Vitas fashion, he paid for the phone - I didn't have any money or credit cards on me at the time. Then we went back to Flushing Meadows and I promised him I'd repay him the next time I saw him. A few days passed and I didn't see him again and I then went back home to Paris. The very first time this new phone rings - the very one that Vitas bought me - it's a journalist on the line to tell me that Vitas had died. I couldn't believe it. He had to repeat it several times. I called his mom and sister at once. I had an exhibition match on the day of the funeral so I couldn't go and I really regret that.

Vitas had a tennis court at his house. We'd practice there

for hours. Despite his lifestyle and reputation, Vitas practiced a lot. He had a huge problem with his serve. He didn't know how to serve. The ball toss was wrong and he would try to practice it every day. He never had powerful serve, or one he could rely on. By the end, it did get better but it was never much of a shot. But he was very quick all over the court so he compensated for it.

(Excerpt from "Mr Nastase The Autobiography: Talented, Tempestuous And Totally Talented" Published By Collins Willow.)

Gerulaitis won series 10-1

Year	Tournament	Surface	Round	Winner	Score
1980	Stuttgart Outdoor	Clay	QF	Gerulaitis	6-2 7-5
1979	Dorado Beach	Hard	RR	Gerulaitis	6-3 6-2
1979	Birmingham	Carpet	QF	Gerulaitis	6-2 6-0
1978	Forest Hills WCT	Clay	F	Gerulaitis	6-2 6-0
1978	Monte Carlo WCT	Clay	QF	Gerulaitis	6-3 1-6 6-3
1977	WCT Challenge Cup	Carpet	RR	Nastase	6-5 5-6 6-4
1977	Houston WCT	Hard	SF	Gerulaitis	4-1 RET

1977 Ocean City   Hard   SF   Gerulaitis   1-6 6-2 6-4

1976 Toronto Indoor WCT   Carpet   SF Gerulaitis 6-3 6-3

1975 Bermuda   Clay   SF   Gerulaitis   1-6 6-2 6-0

1975 Salisbury   Carpet   SF   Gerulaitis   4-6 6-3 6-2 6-1

Nancy Gill McShea: Fan favorite VITAS GERULAITIS passed away Sept. 17, 1994. When we inducted Vitas into the 1995 USTA Eastern Hall of Fame, I asked the newspaper reporter MIKE LUPICA, a friend of Vitas, for permission to print his beautiful Newsday eulogy rather than write Vitas's profile myself, since I did not know him. Mike agreed. Mary Carillo inducted Vitas, his sister Ruta accepted his award...

A special read.......By Mike Lupica

Excerpted-Newsday Sept. 19, 23, 1994 (Edited by Nancy Gill McShea)

This was such a long time ago, in whatever was the hot Italian restaurant of the moment in London in 1977. Vitas Gerulaitis always knew where the hot place was, where to find the people who wanted to laugh the most and stay up the latest. It was a big group, I remember that, because dinner with Vitas in those days was always dinner for just about everyone. He was always the life of the party.

But he could not make himself the life of the party that June night in 1977. He went through the motions, but his heart wasn't in it, because this was the night after the afternoon when he should have beaten Bjorn Borg at Wimbledon. He sat at the head of the table a long time and somehow kept a smile in place, and finally about 11 o'clock he said he was meeting some people at some hot new club.

He was out of Howard Beach, in Queens, which is not supposed to produce the Wimbledon champion. Howard Beach was not even supposed to produce a player who could chase the great Borg around for five thrilling sets that are still discussed in tennis today. But he had done that. Borg was the defending Wimbledon champion. Vitas was 23 years old and a comer, a tennis celebrity already, not just the life of the party but someone who felt like the life of the sport when he was going good, and he was going good at Wimbledon in 1977.

Vitas had stayed with him until 6-all in the final set. He had run and hit all his shots, and Borg, who would turn out to be one of his best friends, had run and hit all his shots. The tennis was something to see. Vitas had his best shot when he was up a service break early in the fifth set. He had a point to go ahead 4-2. The score was 40-30. He had been coming in hard behind his weak second serve all day and getting away with it.

This time he hesitated. Borg took control…won the match (8-6 in the fifth) and two days later he beat Jimmy Connors in the final.

Vitas didn't know anything about that on this night, in the hot Italian restaurant. He just knew he stayed back when he should have come in. He finally stood up and grabbed the check, because he always did that, too.

"That _____ second serve," he said, putting a smile on

the obscenity. Then his voice dropped, and he dropped the smile, and Vitas Gerulaitis said, "I could have won Wimbledon...Imagine that, me winning Wimbledon."

He threw some money on the table and walked into the London night, alone all of a sudden.

He was born in Brooklyn, raised in Howard Beach, attended Archbishop Molloy High School and even Columbia University for a while. He came from public tennis courts all over the city and Long Island, and the Port Washington Tennis Academy. He owned a mansion in Kings Point once, with all the money you could make from tennis if you could make it to No. 4 in the world, and do it all with style, make the whole thing alive and fun just by showing up. He never won Wimbledon. He won the Australian Open, though. He won the Italian Open. He made it to the finals of the U.S. Open and lost to his pal John McEnroe. He had long blond hair and one of the biggest hearts I have ever known about, and he was my friend.

He is a hundred stories, a thousand stories, from the time he won his first big tournament, the U.S. Pro Indoor. That was in Philadelphia. He came right back to New York and tried to spend all the money on clothes the next afternoon, in about two hours. If you ever knew Vitas Gerulaitis, you understand about the hole cut into tennis...God he was fun.

He beat Borg one time at the Masters tournament when the Masters was still held in New York. I don't recall the exact number, but Borg had beaten him something like 16 times in a row...When he came into the interview area, Vitas looked very grave, very serious. Before a question could be asked, he sat down and pointed a finger at the crowd of reporters and said, "Nobody beats Vitas Gerulaitis 17 times in a row." And brought down the house.

I saw him for the last time during the (1994) U.S. Open final. Now Vitas was a comer in television...So I watched another match with him...And then all these years later, for the first time in a long time, I brought up the Borg match. Vitas smiled.

"I shoulda come in on that second serve," he said.

He should have been 41.

* * * *

John Lloyd stood at the top of the steps outside St. Dominic's Church and watched as the casket slowly came through the double doors. Three of the pallbearers were Bjorn Borg and John McEnroe and Jimmy Connors. There was a time back in 1979 when they were ranked No. 1 and No. 2 and No. 3 in the world. No. 4 was…Vitas Gerulaitis.

"You should have seen Vitas last week in Seattle (at Jimmy Connors' Citibank Champions tour for over-35 world-class players)," John Lloyd said quietly…There was this doubles match, and even with Borg and Connors in it, the show belonged to Gerulaitis.

"After the first set," Lloyd said on the church steps, "I said to Jimmy, The other three of us might as well not be here. This is Vitas' room. And Jimmy said, 'Aren't they all?'"

The last room was a church with a high ceiling at the top

of Anstice Street in Oyster Bay. They had come from tennis and television and New York City nights to mourn Gerulaitis. Mary Carillo, remembering the first time she saw Vitas when they were both teenagers at the Port Academy, said, "I remember this big blond streak. He was the most dazzling thing I'd ever seen."

Mary made the church laugh with stories about Vitas, because he was still in the room and that meant you had to laugh. She told of a pajama party Vitas threw in some Pittsburgh hotel on the occasion of his 21st birthday. Then Jimmy Connors was up there, talking about how Vitas still had the magic with people that he took out of New York and all over the tennis map. A fan once mistook Vitas for Borg, even with Borg in the same elevator. Vitas signed Borg's name and when Connors asked him why later, Vitas grinned and said, "Always give them something to make them happy." Connors finished his eulogy and then cried. Because you also had to cry in Vitas' room at St. Dominic's.

After Ruta Gerulaitis had read a simple prayer for her brother, there was this slight pause...Then the three top guys picked up No. 4, and started down the aisle, all laughter gone now from the church, only memories of laughter left behind..."

Career Highlights

Highest ATP world singles ranking – No. 3 (June 11, 1979). Ranked No. 4 for the year. Singles winner -- Australian Open, 1977; singles finalist – French Open, 1980; singles finalist -- US Open, 1979; singles winner -- Italian Open, 1977, 1979; singles winner-Canadian Championships, 1982; singles winner -- Tournament of Champions, Forest Hills,1980; singles finalist-The Masters, Madison Square Garden, 1979, 1981; doubles winner -- Wimbledon, 1975. Compiled 11-3 singles record in U.S. Davis Cup competition. One of the most consistent players in U.S. tennis history. Ranked in the 10 ten for six years from 1977-1982 and in the top 20 from 1975-1984. Captured 27 career singles titles (in 55 finals) and nine doubles crowns...Ranked No. 17 in Open Era singles titles...After retiring from the pro tour, moved to the television booth to provide color commentary for CBS, USA Network and ESPN...Ran free tennis clinics for inner-city kids in City Parks Department, 1979-1989...Supported numerous other charities, including cancer and the Special Olympics.

Pat Cash: (From his autobiography, 'Pat Cash Uncovered'): Little did I know a party hosted by Vitas Gerulaitis would be an evening that changed my whole life. To me at the time, Vitas was quite simply the man. I'm sure that would be the case for every young buck who played hard, both on and off the court. Nowadays many view him as something of a tragic figure, but I have to disagree. Some people want to have fun their whole lives, and there can be little argument that the boy from Queens packed 80 years into the 40 he spent on this earth.

He knew everybody that it was hip to know. He did everything. He hung out with rock stars like the Rolling Stones and Van Halen. He went to every rock concert. He was a magnet for the world's beautiful women and was welcomed warmly at the door of every nightclub. With the possible exception of Ronald Agenor, he could play guitar better than any tennis player.

A regular criticism of Vitas, usually by the duller people around tennis who didn't really know him, is that he played too much off the court and not enough on it. There is definitely a grain of truth in that assumption, but the records show how gifted he was at the game. Vitas won the Australian Open in 1977, beating John Lloyd in the final at Kooyong. I was twelve at the time, smitten with tennis and quite an impressionable kid. Maybe that's why

I always viewed the guy with such admiration. He had also been runner-up at both the French and US Opens, and had that legendary match against Borg at Wimbledon.

Eventually Vitas saw the consequences of his ways. Things got pretty bad, and for a while Vitas was wasted. Then he got his act together and his appearance improved. He put on some weight and developed a passion, bordering on an obsession, for playing golf every day. He had even contested some tennis exhibitions with the Senior Tour in its formative stages, there was a great chance of making sufficient money to get himself back on an even keel. Then tragedy struck. He died from carbon monoxide poisoning from a faulty gas heater at the house of a friend where he was staying after the US Open.

To me, the day of his death was one of those occasions when you always remember your whereabouts. Everyone knows where they were on September 11 or the day Princess Diana was killed. For me, you can add September 17, 1994 to the list. I was playing a tennis exhibition in Ibiza, and I can't remember being more upset about the loss of a great friend. I didn't go across to New York for the funeral, though in retrospect I wish I had. All the people who knew Vitas only had magnanimous things to say about him, and throughout all his problems, he remained a loving, generous and friendly human being. It was a shame that somebody as good as he was, had to die.

By nature of his big-heartedness, all Vitas' friends have something by which they can remember him, and I am probably luckier than most: I have two of the most beautiful children because it was at another Gerulaitis party, back in Houston when I was in the midst of all my back problems, that I met their mother (Anne-Britt Kristiansen)...

LeRoy Neiman: I remember Vitas telling me, "I could play tennis all day."

Peter Figura: I have two Vitas stories that you may not find them interesting. I remember them so well because of him. He was such a unique human being, making everyone around him feel special. The first time I saw Vitas was during the Canadian Open where he was playing in the legends event.

He was playing doubles with Alex Metreveli. During one of the exchanges, the opponents were running Metreveli all over the court. At that time all the hard courts looked the same - green and red with the court area being green. Metreveli was chasing the balls all over the court, and the opponents won that point. Vitas then made a very loud comment - everyone could hear it – 'Hey Russkie - there is no worse insult than calling someone from Georgia to be Russian - stay in the green....you should know that red is not good for you' - he was referring to the red being a color of the communist Russia. Alex was not too pleased but had to swallow his pride.

Vitas, as you know, was the ultimate crowd pleaser - the number of the female tennis fans that came to the Centre court was higher than ever.

A few points later it was Vitas who was chasing the ball. But he focused on showing his skills, and finally after the over-the-left-shoulder winner, Vitas and Alex won the point. The crowd went really crazy. Vitas turned around, opened up his shoulders and said, again, loud enough so everyone could hear him, 'What can I tell you?
Just another day on the tennis court.'

I can't remember if they won the match or not, but it really did not matter.

Second time I met Vitas was at a charity event in Burlington, Ontario at Cedar Springs. It was in 1994. The charity was CAVEAT (Canadians Against Violence Advocating its Termination) Roy Emerson was the other tennis celebrity.

Prior to the tennis match at the live auction Vitas was doing his best to help raise the funds. At some point, with one of the items Vitas put on a Toronto Maple Leafs jersey, and was walking around, flipping the bottom of the jersey as if he was wearing a miniskirt. The crowd went crazy, and I think they've raised $1,200. The same jersey a week before at a different auction only reached $300.

At the tennis match with Roy Emerson and two local pros Sam Rifaat and Brian Millar, Vitas was doing everything to make it great for the public. But he was also very encouraging to support the local pros. Sam was playing 'out of his mind' and Vitas was applauding him. So was the audience, but Sam could not keep up such a high level for the entire match, and when the audience was disappointed Vitas said loudly, 'How quickly they turned their backs on their own man' - basically saying - support your local guy please because he is a great player, and he is your tennis pro.

Also at the auction Vitas himself bought an Andre Agassi an autographed t-shirt and photo. He paid $500 for those items. Then he quietly went back to the auction table, returned those items he just bought, and said to the ladies who were running the desk, 'Please make those items as a draw for the ball kids.' Kids went totally crazy about the auction - Agassi was the kids' hero during those years.

I was working as a linesperson, and standing next to the auction table. When returning those two items, Vitas said to me, 'Thank you for helping out.' I answered, 'Vitas, people came to see you playing. There is no one in this building, with the exception of my mom, that came here to see me calling the lines.' Vitas had his unforgettable smile, and said, 'Everyone is helping out here, and this is really great.'

And this is how I will always remember him... a great player, but an incredible human being. That gesture with the auction items was very special. I was the only one standing next to the auction desk, so no one else would have noticed. Yet, he made everybody, and the entire event very unique.

Vitas Quotes

1977: "You can 't beat a great player by chipping the ball,

just keeping it in play. (Rod) Laver's told me that a dozen times. (Chuck) McKinley told me the same thing."

"On a big point against the top players, you can't expect them to make a mistake. You have to go out and win the point. And you've got to be aggressive match after match. I've realized that if I ever want to win a major title, four matches don't mean anything. You win four matches at Wimbledon or Forest Hills, you're in the quarterfinals."

"I sold it (my Lamborghini). It was kind of a lemon. Never buy a Lamborghini."

"I don't do anything to show off or impress people, I just like to enjoy myself, and I'm lucky enough to be able to."

"The cars? That's my hobby. It's a sickness. I've got stacks of antique car magazines. I love to hang out in body shops, stuff like that. My father and friends look at me like I'm a sicko. I guess I am. A lot of people give me static about it. They say, 'You haven't won Wimbledon or Forest Hills. Borg doesn't own a Rolls Royce," But I don't buy these things for show."

"When friends of mine are in New York, they're welcome to use the cars. I just built a new tennis court at my house, everybody comes over and uses it. I like to share what I have because I think I'm very fortunate. I've gotten more breaks than most players. I'm making more than a lot of players ranked ahead of me."

"I know I get taken advantage of. People abuse the privilege. My family's always saying, 'Don't you know that when you're nobody again, just hacking around the Bowery looking for a second serve, everybody's going to forget. You'll just be a guy with a name that sounds like a disease.'

"Unfortunately, that's the way life is. I'm not going to change it. You might as well enjoy what you've got while you've got it."

1981 US Open: "There was a time when I began to wonder if all these people who were ragging on me were right. I just wasn't keen for tennis at the beginning of the year. I didn't want to do the work, run down the ball, stay out there when I had to."

"People have written me off, a lot of guys who I thought were my friends have gone out of their way to rip me. So my attitude now is the hell with them."

"I'll take the fine ($500 for skipping press conferences) every time. I don't need the money and I don't need the press, either. If I win the tournament I'll take the $60,000 and give it to some bum on the street or something."

"I'm beyond doing this for the money. I don't have to play all that well to make a lot of money. I'm doing this now for the prestige, that's all. They can fine me all they want."

"I got to Connors, I got to McEnroe but I just couldn't get Borg. It got frustrating. I just got tired of chasing, chasing and not getting there. I took time off because I wanted to get away from tennis for a while and when I came back I didn't have the mental toughness I needed. I started losing matches I had taken for granted and I dropped on the computer."

"I had to decide if I wanted to do the work to come back. I hadn't had Fred Stolle with me for most of the year and that hurt me. Fred was the one who made me work hard, gave me discipline. Now he's back and that makes a difference."

"I've learned a lot about people from this experience. A lot of people who used to come around and slap me on the back and be my buddy changed when my game went down. I don't think I've changed. I don't regret it, though, because I've weeded out a lot of people."

"I've gone back to the drawing board with my game and with my life. I know I'm only going to have a chance to play this game really well for maybe three, four more years and that's all I'm worrying about now."

"I've gone through a period that almost everyone goes through at some point, a lull. I've learned one thing from it: How quickly they forget. I'm past the stage of caring what people think or write about me. Today, when I won, I almost felt like crying out there because it had been so long since I've felt the crowd behind me like that. It was an unreal feeling."

"Coming back when people said I couldn't is a hell of a feeling."

1984 US Open

"Ninety-five of the women can't play. Only five percent can. Seventy-five percent of the men can play. McEnroe can be beaten if he has a bad day. Look at what happened last week. Vijay Amritraj isn't even in his class and he beats John because he played a great match. Something disastrous has to happen to Martina in the morning for her to lose."

"I was in a hole for a little while. I had a few real-estate deals that didn't come through. I'm out of the woods now, so I don't have to play just to make payments."

"Yeah, sometimes I'd hit a shot that I couldn't believe. I was really surprised how my game just came all together because at Wimbledon, I was playing okay not great."

"I'd bet my house (the ATP no. 100 ranked player Derek Tarr) would beat Martina (Navratilova)."

Vitas Stats

Ht: 6-0   Wt: 155

ATP Singles Record: 535-232, 26 titles.

ATP Doubles Record: 168-123, 9 titles.

Career best singles ranking No. 9 in 1978.

Career best doubles ranking No. 16 in 1979

Last ATP Match: 1986 Milan Indoors R32 loss to ATP No. 48 Marian Vajda 36 16

ATP Singles Titles (26)

Year	Titles	Tournaments
1984	1	Treviso (Indoor/Carpet)
1983	1	Basel (Indoor/Hard)

1982 5   Johannesburg (Outdoor/Hard) Melbourne-1 (Indoor/Carpet) Toronto (Outdoor/Hard)

Florence (Outdoor/Clay) Brussels (Indoor/Carpet)

1981 1   Johannesburg-2 (Outdoor/Hard)

1980 3   Melbourne (Indoor/Hard) Stuttgart-2 (Outdoor/Clay) Forest Hills WCT (Outdoor/Clay)

1979 4   Sydney-1 (Indoor/Hard) Kitzbuhel (Outdoor/Clay) Rome (Outdoor/Clay)

Little Rock (Indoor/Hard)

1978 3   Forest Hills WCT (Outdoor/Clay) WCT Finals (Indoor/Carpet) Richmond WCT (Indoor/Carpet)

1977 5   Australian Open-2 (Outdoor/Grass) Perth (Indoor/Carpet) Brisbane (Outdoor/Grass)

Rome (Outdoor/Clay) Ocean City (Indoor/Carpet)

1975 2   St. Louis WCT (Indoor/Carpet) New York (Indoor/Hard)

1974 1   Vienna (Indoor/Hard)

ATP Doubles Titles

1979 1   Little Rock (w/ Vladimir Zednik) (Indoor/Hard)

1978 1   Birmingham WCT (w/ Sandy Mayer) (Indoor/Carpet)

1977 1   Brisbane (w/ Bill Scanlon) (Outdoor/Grass)

1976 2   Fort Worth WCT (w/ Sandy Mayer) (Indoor/Hard) Boca Raton (w/ Clark Graebner) (Outdoor/Clay)

1975 2   Wimbledon (w/ Sandy Mayer) (Outdoor/Grass) Roanoke (w/ Sandy Mayer) (Indoor/Carpet)

1974 2   Salt Lake City (w/ Jimmy Connors) (Indoor/Hard) Roanoke (w/ Sandy Mayer) (Indoor/Carpet)

Vitas Grand Slam Matches

1985

French Open

1R   Boris Becker (30)   L 36 76 16 16

Wimbledon

1R   Peter Fleming (45)   W 62 57 64 36 63

2R   John Sadri (34)   W 57 64 36 76 64

3R   Heinz Gunthardt (56)   L 36 76 16 63 57

US Open

1R   Tarik Benhabiles (88)   W 76 36 75 75

2R   Todd Nelson (173)   W 62 36 62 76

3R   Yannick Noah (6)   L 36 46 36

1984

French Open

1R   Lloyd Bourne (0)   W 36 67 64 64 86

2R Martin Jaite (0) L 36 61 46 36

Wimbledon

1R Tony Giammalva (116) W 36 61 64 67 75

2R Balasz Taroczy (68) W 63 75 46 64

3R Brad Gilbert (45) W 76 61 36 64

R16 John Sadri (76) L 36 57 76 64 36

US Open

1R Derek Tarr (100) W 63 63 63

2R Gianni Ocleppo (59) W 61 64 60

3R Ken Flach (224) W 64 62 46 67 61

R16 Andres Gomez (5) L 46 67 16

1983

Australian Open

1R Bye

2R Zoltan Kuharszky (99) L 16 36 36

French Open

1R   Hans Simonsson   (79)   L   46 26 62 16

Wimbledon

1R   Ramesh Krishnan   (67)   W   57 75 76 57 63

2R   Mark Edmondson   (25)   L   67 57 57

US Open

1R   Marcos Hocevar   (60)   W   36 36 62 75 64

2R   Fritz Buehning   (51)   W   36 61 76 62

3R   Aaron Krickstein   (0)   L   63 63 46 36 46

1982

French Open

1R   Erick Iskersky   (75)   W   67 63 76 63

2R   Bernard Boileau   (0)   W   61 62 60

3R   Heinz Gunthardt   (42)   W   62 76 57 64

R16 Mel Purcell (30)   W 63 63 62

QF Mats Wilander (18) L 36 36 64 46

Wimbledon

1R Brent Pirow (0)   W 64 61 61

2R Bruce Derlin (0) W 75 62 63

3R Tomas Smid (26) W 67 36 63 64 62

R16 Roscoe Tanner (25) W 63 64 63

QF Mark Edmondson (19) L 67 63 46 36

US Open

1R Fritz Buehning (56) L 46 67 36

1981

French Open

1R Ricardo Ycaza (59) L 64 26 57 57

Wimbledon

1R Glen Holroyd (0)   W   63 64 76

2R Kevin Curren (34)   W   63 67 63 63

3R Victor Amaya (35)   W   46 64 36 63 75

R16 Bjorn Borg (1)   L 67 57 67

US Open

1R Terry Moor (45)   W   46 63 60 36 62

2R Alejandro Cortes (0)   W   75 60 61

3R Harold Solomon (19)   W   63 62 63

R16 Ivan Lendl (3)   W   63 64 36 36 64

QF Bruce Manson (74)   W   64 62 46 61

SF John McEnroe (1)   L   75 36 26 64 36

1980

French Open

1R Peter Elter (0)   W   16 61 57 62 62

2R Fritz Buehning (93)   W   61 62 61

3R Stanislav Birner (86)   W   61 46 62 61

R16 Ferdi Taygan (88)   W 63 75 61

QF Wojtek Fibak (18)   W   63 57 64 36 63

SF Jimmy Connors (3)   W   61 36 67 62 64

F   Bjorn Borg (1) L 46 16 26

Wimbledon

1R   Stefan Simonsson (96)   W 60 64 62

2R   Sashi Menon (0)   W 67 64 75 62

3R   Bruce Manson (62)   W   64 46 75 64

R16 Wojtek Fibak (18)   L 63 64 36 36 68

US Open

1R Vince Van Patten (47) W   63 64 60

2R   Hank Pfister (40) L 36 26 63 61 67

1979

French Open

1R Butch Walts (42)   W   26 26 63 62 62

2R   Brad Rowe (0)   W   64 61 62

3R   Sandy Mayer (24)   W   61 61 62

R16 Ivan Lendl (47)   W   62 61 63

QF   Jose Higueras (10) W   61 36 64 64

SF   Bjorn Borg (2)   L   26 16 06

Wimbledon

1R   Pat Dupre (37)   L   67 36 63 63 36

US Open

1R   Mark Edmondson (72)   W   63 62 75

2R   Ferdi Taygan (100)   W   62 63 63

3R   Stan Smith (22)   W   76 76 63

R16 Jose Luis Clerc (13) W   76 62 62

QF   Johan Kriek (29)   W   57 63 64 63

SF   Roscoe Tanner (4)   W   36 26 76 63 63

F   John McEnroe (3)   L   57 36 36

1978

Wimbledon

1R Heinz Gunthardt (61)   W 62 62 46 61

2R Jay Royappa (0)   W 63 75 62

3R Sherwood Stewart (84)   W 98 60 62

R16 Hank Pfister (39)   W 63 36 62 63

QF Brian Gottfried (5)   W 75 46 97 62

SF Jimmy Connors (1)   L 79 26 16

US Open

1R Pascar Portes (0)   W 75 75

2R Victor Amaya (34)   W 62 67 63

3R Andrew Pattison (0)   W 64 36 75

R16 Bob Lutz (30)   W 46 64 63 64

QF Johan Kriek (67)   W 62 61 62

SF Bjorn Borg (2) L 36 26 67

1977

Wimbledon

1R Tom Gorman (50)   W   61 98 63

2R Gene Mayer (78)   W   63 61 61

3R Jonathan Smith (0)   W   63 86 64

R16 Dick Stockton (11)   W   61 64 36 64

QF Billy Martin (75)   W   62 89 62 62

SF Bjorn Borg (2)   L   46 63 36 63 68

US Open

1R Patrice Dominguez (0)   W 62 60

2R Tomas Smid (80)   W   62 76

3R John Yuill (81)   W   75 61

R16 Harold Solomon (12)   L   67 36

Australian Open

1R John Marks (0)   W   75 60 61

2R Brad Drewett (0)   W   64 63 63

R16 Dick Bornstedt (0)   W   64 64 64

QF Ray Ruffels (0) W 67 64 64 62

SF John Alexander (23) W 61 62 64

F John Lloyd (51) W 63 76 57 36 62

1976

Wimbledon

1R Milan Holecek (0) W 75 61 75

2R Mark Cox (55) W 63 64 64

3R Steve Krulevitz (0) W 62 62 61

R16 Arthur Ashe (3) W 46 89 64 63 64

QF Raul Ramirez (10) L 64 46 26 46

US Open

1R Bruce Manson (0) W 64 61

2R Steve Krulevitz (98) W 62 62

3R Zelkjo Franulovic (50) W 46 63 62

R16 Jimmy Connors (1) L 46 36 16

1975

Wimbledon

1R Ray Ruffels (69) L   63 46 26 63 16

US Open

1R   Joaquim Rasgado (0) W 57 63 62

2R   Francois Jauffret (46) L 67 57

1974

Wimbledon

1R Karl Meiler (37)   L 86 46 26 16

US Open

1R John Feaver (125) W   36 63 76 61

2R   Arthur Ashe (9) L   67 57 26

1973

US Open

1R John Alexander (32) L   67 67 46

1972

US Open

1R   Vijay Amritraj (0)   W   26 63 62 63

2R   Charlie Pasarell (0) L   67 36 26

1971

US Open

1R   Toshiro Sakai   (0) L 46 62 61 46 61

Mark "Scoop" Malinowski was born in Philadelphia, PA and first attended the US Open in 1989 and watched Ivan Lendl beat 19-year-old Jim Courier 61 62 63 in the third round on Louis Armstrong Stadium and McEnroe/Woodforde defeat Evernden/Steeb 63 63 on the old grandstand in doubles with Tatum O'Neal sitting just a few seats away.

By 1992 Scoop started a Biofile interview column in the Morristown Daily Record and attended the Pathmark Classic in Mahwah, NJ which featured Monica Seles. Thirty years later he's authored thirteen tennis books and has written about tennis for Final Magazine, Tennis Magazine, Tennis Week Magazine, Ace Magazine, ATPworldtour.com, Australian Tennis Magazine and many other publications.

Some of the tennis champions he has done Biofile interviews with include Margaret Court, Don Budge, Pete Sampras, Roger Federer, Rafael Nadal, Jimmy Connors, Billie Jean King, Chris Evert, Mats Wilander, Guillermo Vilas, Andres Gomez, Ivan Lendl, Fred Stolle, John Newcombe, Jim Courier, Yevgeny Kafelnikov, Stan Wawrinka, Martina Hingis, Venus Williams, Maria Bueno, Virginia Wade, Virginia Ruzici, Michael Chang, Marat Safin, Andy Murray, Juan Martin Del Potro, Gustavo Kuerten, Goran Ivanisevic, Sergi Bruguera, John McEnroe, Roy Emerson, Jack Kramer, Petr Korda, Gaston Gaudio, Marin Cilic, Patrick Rafter, Carlos Moya, Stefan Edberg, Ana Ivanovic, Vika Azarenka, Flavia Pennetta, Francesca Schiavone, Ash Barty, Mary Pierce, Manuel Santana, Juan Carlos Ferrero, Johan Kriek, Roscoe Tanner, Arthur Ashe, Andy Roddick, Stan Smith, Richard Krajicek, Pat Cash, Marion Bartoli, Sam Stosur, Conchita Martinez, Barbora Krejcikova, Simona Halep.

Thanks to Rob Glickman for the inspiration, and Fred Stolle, Brian Gottfried, Robert Palmer, John Rast, Dan McClure, Rick Fagel, John James, Don Petrine, John McEnroe, Hans Gildemeister, Joy DeVijon, Barry Beck, Leif Shiras, Andres Gomez, Pat Cash, Ilie Nastase, Jimmy Connor, Bjorn Borg and everybody for their Vitas memories. And special thanks to Fred Mullane for the fabulous cover photo. And thanks to the ATP World Tour,

Miami Open, Newport Hall of Fame Championships, Elizabeth Moore Sarasota Open Challenger, Tallahassee Challenger for media access.

Scoop Malinowski's Books...

Nick Bollettieri: Godfather of Modern Tennis

Facing Federer

Facing Nadal

Facing McEnroe

Facing Andy Murray

Facing Hewitt

Facing Sampras

Facing Marat Safin

Facing Serena Williams/Steffi Graf (Double book)

Close Encounters With Donald Trump

The Book Of Joy

Facing Guillermo Vilas

Marcelo Rios: The Man We Barely Knew

Muhammad Ali: Portrait of a Champion

Heavyweight Armageddon: The Tyson vs Lewis Heavyweight Championship Battle

Facing Bob Probert

80's Hockey Biofiles

Facing Bjorn Borg

Facing Novak Djokovic

Facing Monica Seles

Printed in Dunstable, United Kingdom

77944686R00077